Windows® Phone 7
Application Development
FOR
DUMMIES®

by Bill Hughes and Indrajit Chakrabarty

WILEY

Wiley Publishing, Inc.

Windows® Phone 7 Application Development For Dummies®

Published by
Wiley Publishing, Inc.
111 River Street
Hoboken, NJ 07030-5774

www.wiley.com

WILEY

About the Authors

Bill Hughes: Bill is an experienced marketing strategy executive with over two decades of experience in sales, strategic marketing, and business development roles at several leading corporations, including Microsoft, IBM, General Electric, Motorola, and US West Cellular.

Recently, Bill has worked with Microsoft to enhance its marketing to mobile application developers. He also has led initiatives to develop new products and solutions with several high-tech organizations, including Nextel, Motorola, SBC, and Tyco Electronics.

Bill has been a professor of marketing at the Kellogg School of Management at Northwestern University, where he taught business marketing to MBA students. In his lectures, he presented his findings on the validity of the market research information used in financial analysis. Bill has written articles on this subject for several wireless industry trade magazines. He also has contributed to articles in *USA Today* and *Forbes,* based upon his research reports written for In-Stat, where he was a principal analyst covering the wireless industry, specializing in smartphones and business applications of wireless devices. His most popular studies include "The Symbian Foundation: A Battle Royal for the Ecosystem," "Wireless Data in the Enterprise: The Hockey Stick Arrives," and "Cellphone Trends in U.S. Enterprises: A Small Step from Personal Wireless."

Bill graduated with honors with an MBA from the Kellogg School of Management at Northwestern University and earned a bachelor of science degree with distinction from the College of Engineering at Cornell University, where he was elected to the Tau Beta Pi Engineering Honorary.

He lives in Bellevue, Washington, with his wife, Susan, and three sons, Ellis, Arlen, and Quinlan.

Indrajit Chakrabarty: Indy is a software architect and developer with over 15 years of experience working in several multinational corporations around the world. He is a self-confessed techie and geek, working extensively with the latest technologies from Microsoft such as ASP.NET MVC, Windows Presentation Foundation (WPF), Silverlight, and Windows Phone 7.

Indy currently works as a consultant on Microsoft .NET and Voice over IP (VoIP). He is the owner and principal of a Micro-ISV, Liana Solutions (www.lianasolutions.com), and is available for consulting opportunities around the world.

Indy lives in Sydney, Australia, with his wife, Tiya, and daughter, Liana. He is often seen taking photographs of landscapes and flying around the countryside in single-prop aircrafts.

Dedication

I would like to dedicate this book to my late mother, Marcia G. Hughes, M.D.

—Bill Hughes

I would like to dedicate this book to my lovely ladies, Tiya and Liana.

—Indy Chakrabarty

Authors' Acknowledgments

We need to thank a number of people who helped make this book a reality. First, we want to thank the team at Wiley Publishing, including our acquisitions editor, Katie Mohr, and our project editor and copy editor, Elizabeth Kuball; we sincerely hope that your patience is rewarded. We also want to thank Steve Ballmer for his support in getting the attention needed to get this book off top dead center.

Bill would like to thank his literary agent, Carole Jelen, of Waterside Publishing, for her support, encouragement, knowledge, and negotiation skills.

Indy would like to thank Bill, for accepting him as a co-author and mentoring him throughout the project. He would also like to thank Carole Jelen, of Waterside Publishing, for introducing him to Bill and Wiley and for helping him with the formalities.

Publisher's Acknowledgments

We're proud of this book; please send us your comments at http://dummies.custhelp.com. For other comments, please contact our Customer Care Department within the U.S. at 877-762-2974, outside the U.S. at 317-572-3993, or fax 317-572-4002.

Some of the people who helped bring this book to market include the following:

Acquisitions and Editorial

Project Editor: Elizabeth Kuball

Senior Acquisitions Editor: Katie Mohr

Copy Editor: Elizabeth Kuball

Technical Editor: McClellan C. Francis

Editorial Manager: Jodi Jensen

Editorial Assistant: Amanda Graham

Senior Editorial Assistant: Cherie Case

Cover Photos: © istockphoto.com / Nataliia Fedori; © istockphoto.com / ReneeKeith; © istockphoto.com / poco_bw; © istockphoto.com / quavondo; © istockphoto.com / Aldo Murillo; © istockphoto.com / Lise Gagne; © istockphoto.com / Patrick Robbins; © istockphoto.com / Kevin Russ; © istockphoto.com / eva serrabassa; ©istockphoto.com / Aldo Murillo; © istockphoto.com / Pavel Losevsky; © istockphoto.com / Michael DeLeon; © istockphoto.com / Marcus Lindström; © istockphoto.com / AVTG; © istockphoto.com / Daniel Bendjy; © istockphoto.com / jeffrey shanes

Cartoons: Rich Tennant (www.the5thwave.com)

Composition Services

Project Coordinator: Katherine Crocker

Layout and Graphics: Claudia Bell, Samantha K. Cherolis, Joyce Haughey, Corrie Socolovitch

Proofreaders: Lindsay Amones, Kathy Simpson

Indexer: Estalita Slivoskey

Publishing and Editorial for Technology Dummies

Richard Swadley, Vice President and Executive Group Publisher

Andy Cummings, Vice President and Publisher

Mary Bednarek, Executive Acquisitions Director

Mary C. Corder, Editorial Director

Publishing for Consumer Dummies

Kathy Nebenhaus, Vice President and Executive Publisher

Composition Services

Debbie Stailey, Director of Composition Services

Contents at a Glance

√

Table of Contents

Introduction

. . . .

*W*indows Phone 7 is a revolutionary cellular operating system that sets a new standard for convenience and productivity. It can integrate with your personal and work computers better than any other phone currently on the market. It works closely with three excellent Microsoft services: Windows Live, Xbox Live, and Zune. Finally, Windows Phone 7 runs a variety of mobile applications. But no matter how many apps there are today (and there are lots!), there's always room for more. And this is where you — and this book — come in.

About This Book

The purpose of this book is to get you started writing applications for Windows Phone 7. We can't guarantee that the applications you write will achieve commercial success, but we can get you through the development process as easily as possible so that you can compete in the marketplace of new ideas.

Keep in mind that this book is a reference — you don't have to read it from beginning to end to get all you need out of it. The information is clearly organized and easy to access. You don't need thick glasses to understand *Windows Phone 7 Application Development For Dummies.* This book helps you figure out what you want to do — and then tells you how to do it, in plain English.

Conventions Used in This Book

We don't use many conventions in this book, but there are a few you should know about:

- ✔ Whenever we introduce a new term, we put it in *italics* and define it shortly thereafter (often in parentheses).

- ✔ We use **bold** for the action parts of numbered steps, so you can easily see what you're supposed to do.

- ✔ We use `monofont` for web addresses and e-mail addresses, so they stand out from the surrounding text. *Note:* When this book was printed, some web addresses may have needed to break across two lines of text. If that happened, rest assured that we haven't put in any extra characters (such as hyphens) to indicate the break. So, when using one of these web addresses, just type in exactly what you see in this book, as though the line break doesn't exist.

✓ We call the device (the phone itself) the Windows Phone, and we call the platform that the phone runs on Windows Phone 7.

What You're Not to Read

We think you'll find every last word of this book scintillating, but we may be a little biased. The truth is, you don't have to read the following:

✓ **Sidebars:** Sidebars are the gray boxes throughout the book. They're interesting but not essential to the topic at hand, so if you're short on time or you only want the information you absolutely need, you can skip them.

✓ **Text marked with the Technical Stuff icon:** For more on this icon, see the "Icons Used in This Book" section, later in this Introduction.

Foolish Assumptions

You know what they say about assuming, so we don't do much of it in this book. But we do make a few assumptions about you:

✓ **You have a Windows Phone.** You may be thinking about buying a Windows Phone, but our money's on your already owning one. After all, getting your hands on the phone is the best way to really understand its capabilities.

✓ **You're at least somewhat familiar with programming.** You may not be a professional programmer, but you've at least created a simple program in the past. If you're totally new to programming, this book still has something to offer you — but you'll have an easier time of it if you've done a little programming in the past.

How This Book Is Organized

The 23 chapters in this book are divided into seven parts. Here's what you can find in each part.

Part I: So, You Want to Develop a Windows Phone App

The first part of this book gets you familiar with the basic capabilities of the Windows Phone 7 platform and introduces the steps involved in getting an app developed and launched.

Chapter 1 provides an overview of the book. Chapter 2 introduces some of the basics of the new Windows Phone 7 platform and gets you up to speed on what's special about the platform. Chapter 3 gets PC programmers familiar with some of the considerations for writing apps in the mobile environment. And Chapter 4 covers the preparations you should make before you begin programming.

Part II: Assembling the Tools You Need as a Developer

In this part, we walk you through the steps to get the tools you need to create applications for the Windows Phone 7 platform, as well as the resources you can access for more information. Believe it or not, we can't cover everything you may ever need for programming on the Windows Phone 7 platform. But we do the next-best thing and tell you where to find the information you need quickly and easily.

Chapter 5 covers the steps for downloading the tools you need to begin application development. Chapter 6 presents the extensive array of reference tools that are available for you in the Microsoft Developer Portal. In Chapter 7, we introduce Silverlight, the development environment intended for applications running on Windows Phone 7.

Part III: Practicing with Simple Sample Apps

The best way to learn to program is to get some practice with simple (but not *too* simple) applications. If you've been programming for years on other platforms, this part is still useful — it gives you information on how the development tools work.

Okay, so maybe the app in Chapter 8 is too simple. But the idea is to get you over the challenge of using Visual Studio by introducing a simple app so you can focus on the other aspects of working with the tools.

In Chapter 9, you create a simple calculator. This time you create a simple app that can have value as a stand-alone application.

Chapter 10 walks you through creating another simple app, but it involves using information from the Internet.

Chapter 11 interacts with the powerful multimedia apps that are incorporated into the Windows Phone. This is good practice in following the guidelines required by Microsoft for the acceptance of apps into the Marketplace.

Part IV: Getting Fancy with APIs

Some of the practice apps in Part III use information from the phone and do things to phone settings based upon instructions you program. This involves interacting with application programming interfaces (APIs).

Chapter 12 interacts with the accelerometer — a very convenient way to make applications interesting and convenient.

Another unique capability within mobile phones is the ability to incorporate location-based services, and Chapter 13 offers you experience in working with these capabilities.

Phones, unlike most PCs, can be turned sideways and upside-down. Chapter 14 orients you to the phone's orientation.

Chapter 15 explores push notification, the way in which Windows Phone 7 alerts the user to updates.

Part V: Leveraging the Windows Phone Marketplace

The best (and only) place to sell your application is the Windows Phone Marketplace. Each and every application, including each revision, goes through an approval process before being allowed on a phone. The goal of Chapter 16 is to make this approval process as easy as possible.

Chapter 17 gives you the tools you need to help your app stand out in the crowd. You'll probably have lots of competition, so you want to put your best foot forward to get the attention your app deserves.

People use Windows Phone devices in dozens of countries, and you'll need to decide which countries you want to offer your app in by translating your app into the local language and pricing in the local currency. Chapter 18 outlines what you need to consider when taking your app global, as well as the steps to make it work.

Chapter 19 covers how to get paid (assuming that you aren't giving away your work for free). You can just let Microsoft do all the calculations, or you can try to understand how they calculate your share of the revenue. In this part, we give you the information you need.

Part VI: A Designer's Work Is Never Done: Updates and Customer Service

It would be nice if all you had to do was count the royalty checks after your app is out on the Marketplace. However, refreshing your app with new capabilities keeps the royalty checks from disappearing. In Chapter 20, we walk you through updating your app.

Those darn customers sometimes have problems and expect you to help. Trust us: You'll want to help them. Chapter 21 explains some best practices.

Part VII: The Part of Tens

This wouldn't be a *For Dummies* book without a Part of Tens. Chapter 22 covers ten features to look for in future Windows Phone releases. In Chapter 23, you find ten ways to make your app more successful.

Icons Used in This Book

Throughout this book, we use *icons* (little pictures in the margin) to draw your attention to various types of information. Here's a key to what those icons mean:

This whole book is like one series of tips. When we share especially useful tips and tricks, we mark them with the Tip icon.

This book is a reference, which means you don't have to commit it to memory — there is no test at the end. But once in a while, we do tell you things that are so important that we think you should remember them, and when we do, we mark them with the Remember icon.

Whenever you may do something that could cause a major headache, we warn you with the, er, Warning icon.

We use the Technical Stuff icon to flag material that's a bit more detailed than you actually need to perform the task at hand. If you're the kind of person who likes to know the *why* and not just the *what,* you'll find Technical Stuff paragraphs fascinating. If not, rest assured that you can safely skip these paragraphs without missing anything essential to your understanding of the material.

Where to Go from Here

If you've never written a program before, you probably want to start with Part I and read through the book from beginning to end.

If you're an experienced programmer who has worked with other mobile platforms, Parts I and II will familiarize you with the Windows Phone 7 platform and the tools at your disposal. Then jump into whichever chapter tickles your fancy or answers your questions. Skim Part III and maybe Part IV, if you want to get to know the APIs used in the sample apps. Otherwise, you may find it quicker to go to the sources described in Chapter 6.

Regardless of your experience level, use the table of contents and index to locate the information you need.

Part I

So, You Want to Develop a Windows Phone App

In this part . . . .

The Windows Phone 7 platform is a new environment for users and prospective application developers. In this part, we fill you in on the capabilities of the platform and prepare you with the information you need before diving into the nitty-gritty of mobile application development. Whether this is your first time programming or you're an old hand, the chapters in this part give you the information you need to get started.

Photo credits: PhotoDisc, Inc. (top); Digital Vision (middle); Purestock (bottom)

Developing an App for Windows Phone 7: An Overview

In This Chapter

▶ Developing apps for Windows Phone 7

▶ Taking care of your customers after the app is in their hands

*T*he approach Microsoft has taken with its Windows Phone 7 platform is very different from its approach with Windows Mobile. The Windows Mobile platform was targeted primarily toward businesses; the secondary audience was consumers who liked its computerlike user interface. The Windows Phone 7 platform, on the other hand, is targeted toward consumers with the expectation that employee demand, combined with some business-friendly features, will bring this device into the corporate environment.

Many professional app developers wrote apps for the Windows Mobile platform, now called Windows Phone Classic, under the proprietary specifications of companies for their employees. Sales volumes of the Windows Mobile platform grew in triple digits in the middle of the last decade. It competed well with the other smartphones available at the time, such as the BlackBerry and the Palm Treo.

The overall smartphone marketplace, loosely defined as cellphones that could run third-party applications with the option of a mobile data connection for real-time updates, was growing very quickly. However, none of the existing competitors had the buzz that was seen when Apple announced its iPhone.

Digital Vision

Initially, the iPhone was not technically a smartphone, because it didn't accept third-party applications. But it came with enough cool apps to capture the imagination of consumers. Soon thereafter, Apple announced its iPhone Software Development Kit (SDK), and then the App Store, where consumers could acquire apps for their iPhone. This announcement drew a great response from professional and nonprofessional developers alike; they generated apps to address problems many consumers didn't even know they had!

Many phone manufacturers raced their iPhone-killing phones to the market, but what really turned the tide was Google's announcement about its Android smartphone platform. This was to be a virtual developer's paradise, with extensive support tools and less bureaucracy than developers have to go through to get apps launched on the Apple App Store.

Nothing riles the folks in Redmond, Washington, more than a competitive challenge, particularly in a marketplace that they believe should've been theirs in the first place. To respond to the iPhone and Android, Microsoft decided to start over with a new approach to mobile phones. Among its key strategic decisions for the phone:

- ✓ **Standardize on the best hardware.** Microsoft believed that it lost control of how handset manufacturers were implementing Windows Mobile hardware, causing an unstable environment and an inconsistent user experience. No more. There are two screen sizes, and the processor and graphics processing unit (GPU) are state of the art and must be used by all manufacturers. This makes the life of a programmer easier.

- ✓ **Leverage successful Microsoft platforms.** In addition to the basics of phone calling, texting, and wireless e-mail, Microsoft believed that it could make its phone stand out by leveraging its other successful product lines. Windows Phone 7 uses "hubs" that give you convenient access to the Microsoft services, allowing you to bring your work and home computing together on the Windows Phone 7 platform when you're on the go.

- ✓ **Use familiar development tools.** Many, if not most, application developers have used Microsoft development tools. Microsoft has charged for these tools in the past, but to make it more appealing for nonprofessional developers, it's offering a free version specifically for Windows Phone 7 users.

We explore each of these approaches in more detail in this chapter and later chapters.

Knowing the Tools You Need

Regardless of your experience as a developer, you need certain tools to get started developing apps for Windows Phone 7. The basic tools are free, and we cover these in Chapter 5. If you want to get fancier, you can buy tools. We walk you through the steps to figure out what's useful and download what you need.

Microsoft also provides Windows Phone 7 app developers oodles of technical manuals, blogs, reference sites, videos, podcasts, and code samples. Chapter 6 introduces some of the most valuable tools in that "virtual library" known as the Microsoft Developer Portal. More important, we tell you where to find what you need as you need it.

We dedicate Chapter 7 to Silverlight, the environment for applications. Silverlight is very convenient and powerful, and we go into detail on its capabilities.

Developing a Basic App

If you're new to developing apps, we get you off and running in Part III, developing some basic apps. These apps are really closer to *widgets,* small apps that do one thing and are almost always free. This part is all about getting you comfortable with the app development process.

If you're an experienced programmer, you may want to skip or just skim Part III.

Taking It Up a Notch

Starting with Part IV, we explore slightly more sophisticated applications.

Chapter 12 introduces the *accelerometer* (a sensor that measures how fast the phone is moving); Chapter 13 is all about using location services that are on the Windows Phone; and Chapter 14 covers the sensors that use the phone's orientation. Using these application programming interfaces (APIs) not only makes for interesting apps, but also gets you used to using any API that's in the library.

Why develop for Windows Phone 7?

There are numerous smartphone platforms, each with a pitch for why you, a prospective developer, should want to write for that platform. In the mobile space, in addition to Windows Phone 7, you can write apps for the following platforms:

- **iOS from Apple for the iPhone:** Development on Apple's iOS is considered by experienced programmers to be harder to learn. This is an important consideration for novice programmers. Plus, there are over 300,000 apps in the Apple App Store. It is hard to stand out among that much inventory.

- **Android from Google:** Google positioned its Android platform as being programmer-friendly, even more than being user-friendly. This has made it very popular among developers. Although Apple has the largest number of apps in its marketplace, Android is growing at a faster pace.

- **webOS from Hewlett-Packard:** webOS has a great legacy with its origins as Palm. It isn't clear how HP will leverage this legacy. HP is considered a great hardware company, but its reputation in software is mixed (and that's putting it politely).

- **BlackBerry OS from Research In Motion:** Research In Motion was promoting its application development for years before Apple launched the first iPhone, and it still hasn't caught on. Many people find the application development environment to be even more restrictive than Apple's, and many developers complain loudly about that.

Microsoft offers several advantages for its developers:

- **The development tools and systems used for Windows Phone 7 are the same ones that are used for PCs.** Although Apple has grown recently, Microsoft still sells eight or nine copies of Windows for every copy of Mac OS X.

- **The development environment used for the Windows Phone 7 is Silverlight.** (Games can be developed in XNA, but we don't go into detail on that in this book). Silverlight application skills can be leveraged in other environments.

- **The support of SharePoint is unique among smartphones.** The Mobile Office apps are better than other options. This makes the Windows Phone a strong competitor for heavy business users and in situations where an enterprise buys phones for its employees.

- **At the same time, Windows Phone 7 is a strong competitor for gamers.** Although the stereotype of gamers is different from that of enterprise users, Xbox LIVE fans will be drawn to using the Windows Phone 7 platform.

Microsoft has invested a great deal in making the Windows Phone 7 platform a success, and it isn't done yet. You have a chance to get in on the ground floor by developing for Windows Phone 7. And this book gives you the tools you need.

Chapter 15 explores the Microsoft Push Notification Service within Windows Phone 7. This is an important subject if your app will ever need to communicate with apps or websites off the phone. If your app is entirely self-contained on the phone (like a calculator), you don't need to use push notification. But if you want to get real-time information or to grab data from a website, push notification is the tool you use.

Selling Your App

Unless you select a narrowly defined target market for your handiwork and market it, the only customers you'll get are your friends and family. You need to find a way to get your apps noticed.

The Windows Marketplace offers some options to help your app be sorted correctly and made available in multiple geographic markets. Part V of this book walks you through this process.

You may be fine with developing free apps, but if you want to be compensated for all your hard work, you'll find Chapter 19 particularly useful.

Following Through

You'll definitely want to offer updates to your customers. Chapter 20 tells you how to let your current customers know that you have a new and improved version.

You also need a way to support your customers if they have questions. You can do it on the cheap, or you can slather your customers with love and attention. What you can't do is ignore customers with questions — unless you never want to sell another app. In Chapter 21, we fill you in on how to keep your customers satisfied.

2

A Windows Phone 7 Primer

*B*efore we get into how to program for the Windows Phone, it would be helpful to describe the environment. We start with the hardware. After all, the buttons and hardware affect what you can do. Then we cover the hubs that are an integral part of the Windows Phone 7 platform. And we end with the apps that are already on the phone. There's no sense in your duplicating what's already there, but you may want to write apps that enhance some of the built-in apps.

Meet the Hardware

When planning your Windows Phone 7 application, you need to be aware of the hardware on the Windows Phone. The Windows Phone has some of the best and fastest hardware out there.

Courtesy of Microsoft Corporation

The hardware buttons

The Windows Phone has seven hardware buttons (see Figure 2-1):

- ✔ **Power:** The Power button turns the phone on, puts it in sleep mode, or shuts it down. What it does depends upon whether the phone is off and how long you press it.

- ✔ **Camera:** This button opens the Camera application.

 ✔ **Volume Up/Down:** These two buttons turn up the volume of the ringer, the music, or your app.

 ✔ **Windows:** This button takes you to the Start screen with the tiles from wherever you are in an application.

 ✔ **Back:** This button takes you back one screen or one level, depending on the nature of the application you're using.

 ✔ **Search:** This button allows you to search based upon the context of what you're doing. For example, if you're on the Start screen, pressing the Search button initiates a Bing search. If you're in an application, pressing the Search button will search within that app. If you design your app so that it's searchable, this is the button the user will press to initiate a search.

Volume Up/Down

Power

Camera

Back   Windows   Search

Courtesy of Samsung

Figure 2-1: Buttons on a typical Windows Phone 7.

The touchscreen

In addition to the hardware buttons, Microsoft uses a multitouch screen on the Windows Phone 7 with 800-x-480-pixel resolution. There are several gestures that you should know, because they may be useful in your app:

- ✔ **Tap (see Figure 2-2):** The tap gesture launches a function. This gesture is the equivalent of the double-click on a PC mouse.

- ✔ **Double tap (see Figure 2-3):** If your application has zoomed in or panned out, the double tap reverses that action.

- ✔ **Pinch and stretch (see Figure 2-4):** If your application needs to zoom in or out on an image, you use these gestures. Putting two fingers on the screen and pinching them zooms out. Putting two fingers on the screen and stretching them apart zooms in.

Finger down on a single point within a bounded area and back up within a short period of time.

Figure 2-2: The tap gesture.

Two quick taps within a bounded area.

Figure 2-3: The double-tap gesture.

✔ **Pan (see Figure 2-5):** This gesture involves putting your finger on the screen and dragging it to move the image on the screen. It's the equivalent of a scroll on a PC.

✔ **Flick (see Figure 2-6):** Flicking the screen also pans the image, only faster.

The software keyboard

When the user taps a text box, Windows Phone 7 brings up a software keyboard (see Figure 2-7). The only time the software keyboard doesn't appear is when there is a hardware keyboard on the phone and the hardware keyboard is extended.

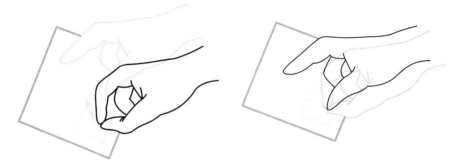

Figure 2-4: The pinch gesture zooms out (left), and the stretch gesture zooms in (right).

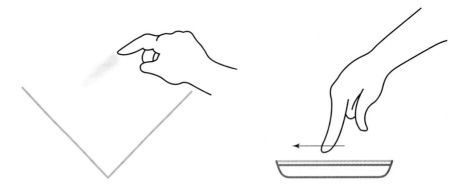

Finger down followed by finger move in a single direction or multiple directions. Pan ends on finger up (or when another gesture starts).

Figure 2-5: The pan gesture for controlled movement.

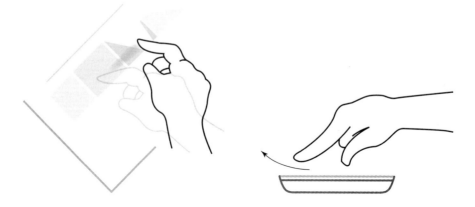

Finger down followed by a quick finger move in a single
direction and finger up. Flick can also follow a pan gesture.

Figure 2-6: The flick gesture for faster movement.

Figure 2-7: The software keyboard.

What's under the hood

The Windows Phone comes with an apps processor, a separate graphics processing unit (GPU), and a variety of sensors:

- **The apps processor:** The main apps processor runs at least 1 GHz.

- **The GPU:** Unless you use a liquid-cooled behemoth, the GPU in the Windows Phone is probably more powerful than what you have in your PC. Plus, it sips only a tiny fraction of the power of a PC-based GPU.

- **The sensors:** There are six sensors on the phone that stand ready to provide you information through application programming interfaces (APIs). They include the following:

  - **Accelerometer:** The accelerometer can sense the special orientation and movement of the phone. It can tell your app when the phone is being tilted, shaken, or stirred.

  - **A-GPS:** In addition to the GPS chip, which picks up the GPS satellites, the phone is assisted (hence, the "A-") by knowing its location relative to cell towers. This information helps determine where the phone is on a map a bit faster.

  - **Proximity sensor:** The proximity sensor tells the phone when it's close to an object. The primary use of this sensor is to turn off the screen when you bring the phone to your ear.

  - **Camera:** Although you can't replace the Camera app on the phone, you can get the image from the camera and use it as you want.

  - **Light:** The light sensor is mainly there to adjust the brightness setting on the screen. This sensor won't do you much good.

  - **Compass:** The initial release of Windows Phone 7 doesn't give you this information. You have to use the mapping application to get started.

The output options

There are three ways you can give user output through APIs:

- **Sound:** You can use either the speaker or the audio output jack.

- **The screen:** You can display text or images.

- **Vibration:** There are APIs to control *haptic feedback* (the buzzing sensation that you get in some higher-end phones to give you a physical sensation that your input has been recognized).

We explore these subjects more in later chapters, but for now just be aware that users can disable the sound and turn off the haptic feedback. If you're counting on either of these output methods being present for your app, you may need to consider what to do if the user shuts them off.

The Hubs Are Where It's At: Navigating on the Windows Phone

The Windows Phone is a smartphone, but it's more than your average smartphone. It has unique capabilities and features that put it in a category all its own. In this section, I fill you in on the details.

People and social networks

One way that Windows Phone is different from other smartphones is the way it allows the user to put all the information on his or her contacts in one spot. There are two ways Windows Phone 7 does this:

- ✔ **Tiles on the Start screen:** The user can set up the Start screen so that each person's image is on his or her unique tile. Then the user simply taps on a person's tile to see all the Facebook and Windows Live messages from and to that person.

- ✔ **The People hub:** The People hub is like a contact database on steroids. A hub is like a personal website where all the sources of information are set up in a format that's easy to view on your Windows Phone. The panorama in Figure 2-8 shows that there are three sections to the People hub:

Courtesy of Microsoft Corporation

Figure 2-8: The People hub.

- **Recent:** All the new contacts who are recently added

- **All:** All friends, new and old

- **What's New:** All the latest social-network updates from all your friends

Whereas you might assign a tile on the Start screen for each of your closest friends or family members, the People hub lets you keep track of all the people you know.

Pictures

The Pictures hub helps you use the digital camera on your Windows Phone to its full potential.

Studies of cellphone users have found that we tend to snap a bunch of pictures on our phones the first month. After that, the photos sit on the phone (instead of being downloaded to our computers), and our picture-taking rate drops dramatically. When we upgrade to new phones, sometimes we lose the photos on our old phones, or only then do we take the time to download the images onto our home computers.

The Windows Phone is different. The Pictures hub (shown in Figure 2-9) allows the user to integrate camera images into a home photo library, as well as photo-sharing sites such as Flickr, with minimal effort. Plus, the user can integrate these photos with the People hub and social-networking sites.

Music and videos

Sure, your Windows Phone can take advantage of all that Zune has to offer. But Windows Phone 7 also has the Music + Videos hub (see Figure 2-10), which offers you more information than just what multimedia files are available on the phone. The Music + Videos hub gives the user quick access to new tracks and the tracks that have been listened to most recently.

Games

In addition to the games that the user can download from the Windows Marketplace, the Windows Phone offers integration with the Microsoft Xbox LIVE website (www.xbox.com). This integration takes place through the Games hub (shown in Figure 2-11).

The Games hub brings all gaming assets together in one spot. The user can access them whether he's on an Xbox console, a computer, or a Windows Phone. No self-respecting Xbox fan will want to use any cellphone other than the Windows Phone.

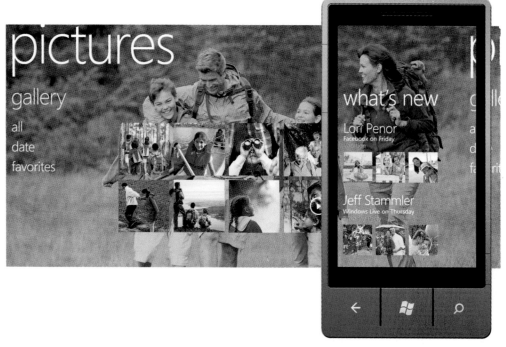

Courtesy of Microsoft Corporation

Figure 2-9: The Pictures hub takes your camera phone to a whole new level.

Courtesy of Microsoft Corporation

Figure 2-10: The Music + Videos hub makes it easier to listen to music and play videos.

Figure 2-11: The Games hub lets you take your Xbox experience mobile.

Business and e-mail

Whether a company gives its employees Windows Phones to use for work or a consumer buys a Windows Phone for personal use and productivity, the Windows Phone Office hub (shown in Figure 2-12) gives the user tools to keep on top of what happens in the office.

The Office hub integrates the information on the Microsoft SharePoint system with the Microsoft Mobile Office applications on your Windows Phone. This allows the user to access the latest version of any Microsoft Office file. In addition, the user can access her office's Outlook e-mail system and integrate it with the e-mail on the Windows Phone. These capabilities are truly unique to the Windows Phone.

Courtesy of Microsoft Corporation

Figure 2-12: The Office hub.

Built-in Applications

As an application developer, you need to know what apps are already on the Windows Phone. Some apps are available on the Start screen. All apps, including those on the Start screen, are listed on the App screen.

Applications on the Start screen

The previous section fills you in on the hubs that are in a panorama that extends beyond the visible screen. The Start screen is similar, but instead of being horizontal, it's vertical (see Figure 2-13). The Start screen has the tiles that you're most likely to tap first. When you first get a Windows Phone, these are all the applications.

Figure 2-13: The full panorama of the Start screen.

The applications accessible from the Start screen include the following:

- **Internet Explorer:** The Internet Explorer that comes standard with the Windows Phone works almost identically to the Internet Explorer that's on your PC. To economize on space, Microsoft has left off many of the programming tools. This doesn't affect your efforts, however, because you'll do your application development on a PC, not on the phone.

You see many familiar toolbars, including Favorites and Search Engine. The mobile version of Internet Explorer also includes tabs that allow you to open multiple Internet Explorer sessions simultaneously.

✔ **Office:** The Microsoft Office applications on the Windows Phone are designed to operate in many of the same ways as their PC counterparts. Unlike Microsoft Office for your PC, which has a list price of almost $400, Office in included on the Windows Phone at no additional charge.

Here are the applications within the Microsoft Office for Mobile suite:

- Microsoft Word
- Microsoft Excel
- Microsoft PowerPoint
- Microsoft OneNote
- Microsoft SharePoint

✔ **Clock:** A very simple application that — drum roll, please — presents the time. In addition to showing the time, the Clock application presents the current time in other world cities. The application has a default display but also gives you options for *skins,* which present the present time using a variety of formats (such as an analog clock face or a digital display).

You can change the Clock to your preference by tapping the ellipsis (. . .) icon at the bottom of the screen.

You can use the ellipsis in your programming to move some of the less frequently used capabilities off the screen. Keep this trick in mind.

✔ **Calendar:** The Windows Phone has a stand-alone Calendar application in which you can set up appointments on your phone. Just tap the Calendar icon, and you see the daily calendar (shown in Figure 2-14). If you prefer to look at your calendar on a monthly basis, you just tap the Month tab on the daily calendar (also shown in Figure 2-14).

You can add an appointment by tapping the plus sign on the screen. This brings up the New Appointment screen, shown in Figure 2-15. Enter the information into each field using the software keyboard, and — *voilà!* — you've scheduled an appointment on your phone.

When the time of an appointment approaches, you'll get a pop-up message like the one shown in Figure 2-16. You can dismiss the notice or tap Snooze to be reminded of the appointment later.

✔ **Calculator:** The calculator (shown in Figure 2-17) is a straightforward algebraic calculator. And that's pretty much all there is to say about it.

✔ **Marketplace:** Marketplace is the Microsoft site where the user can buy your app. We cover this in much more detail in Part V.

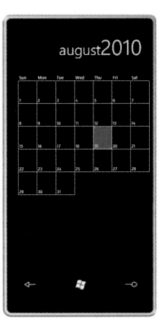

Figure 2-14: The daily and monthly calendars.

Figure 2-15: The New Appointment screen.

Figure 2-16: The screen alerting you to an approaching appointment.

Figure 2-17: The Calculator screen.

These applications are the ones that Microsoft has determined to be the top priority for most Windows Phone users. Different cellular carriers may customize this screen by reprioritizing or adding applications that they see as important.

Take a good look at the screen layout for these applications. These all use a style that Microsoft calls the Metro user interface. They want applications to use these fonts and layout. These are described in the Microsoft document "UI Design and Interaction Guide for Windows Phone 7," available at http://go.microsoft.com/fwlink/?LinkID=183218. (See Chapter 4 for more on the Metro UI.)

More applications

The previous section covers the applications that are on the Start screen. But by flicking the screen one page to the right, you get a complete list of the applications, utilities, and settings on the phone. Figure 2-18 shows the applications in panorama format. Even though this phone is new, the list of applications is extensive — and it'll grow as the user adds more apps.

The applications that are accessible from the Applications screen include (but are not limited to) the following:

- **Alarms:** This application allows you to set a time for an alarm to go off. When you tap the Alarms icon, you get a screen with a list of saved alarm types. This shows the current alarm settings, and each setting has its own name so that you can easily distinguish it.

- **Camera:** The Camera app allows you to take pictures.

- **Convert:** The Convert app is a special-purpose calculator that converts units of measure (such as length, volume, and mass) to other formats. For example, the Convert app can convert meters to feet or pounds to kilograms.

- **Maps:** The Maps application takes you to the Microsoft Bing search engine.

- **Speed Type:** This is a Microsoft application that helps you become more comfortable with the software keyboard. It includes lessons you can complete to improve your typing on a Windows Phone.

Not all phones will come with this entire list. They all have Camera, Maps, and Marketplace. Most have the Alarm app. Beyond that, it's hit or miss. There may be more; there may be fewer.

Figure 2-18: All the applications on the Windows Phone are just a flick away.

3

Getting into the Mobile Apps Environment for Windows Phone 7

*E*ven before planning a new application, you need to scope out the programming environment. Some functions are automated and take place with minimal programming on your part; other functions are prohibited; still others are done in a unique way. For example, you can't dip into the contact database on the phone and start calling telephone numbers — that would make the phone vulnerable to malware or bad programming.

Microsoft has put together a structure for application development that is meant to offer as many capabilities as possible in a first major release within a protected, sandbox environment. Where Microsoft lands with this release is different from earlier versions of the Windows Mobile OS. It's also different from the other mobile OSs that are currently vying for your attention.

The best way to describe the scope of the environment is to explain the capabilities and limitations of the Windows Phone 7 platform. That's what we do in this chapter.

ImageState

The new variation of Windows CE

Windows Phones are based upon the Windows CE operating system (although if they heard us say that, a horde of people at Microsoft would be collectively cringing). But being based on CE is not a bad thing — it's good.

Here's a little background information on Windows CE: The Windows OSs we use on PCs, like Windows 7, are written to run on Intel microprocessor architecture. Historically, the goal of most Intel processors has been performance. Most people like their PCs to run fast. However, fast on an Intel processor, with its architecture, has meant the use of more electrical power.

This isn't a problem on desktops that are plugged into wall sockets. But when it comes to laptops, users accept a compromise: less processing horsepower in exchange for longer battery life and/or a lighter battery.

Here is where Windows CE comes in. In about 1990, a company called Advanced RISC Machines, now called ARM, came up with an architecture for microprocessors that were designed to be powerful yet conserve power. ARM licensed its architecture to other chip makers instead of making the chips itself. ARM-architected chips have become the basis for almost all nonlaptop portable devices, including PDAs, cellphones, and smartphones.

Microsoft came out with Windows CE (short for Compact Edition) in 1996. Windows CE minimizes the need for RAM and power. It can run on both Intel and ARM processors, but it's different from Windows and doesn't run applications written for regular Windows.

This last fact can get confusing when applications like Microsoft Word and Microsoft Word Mobile have nearly identical names and can share files. You can't run Microsoft Word on your phone; neither can you run Microsoft Word Mobile on your PC. Even though they both can work with .doc files, they aren't the same.

Now we get to Windows Phone 7. It's a new environment, although it starts with the same core (called a *kernel*) as Windows Mobile. However, Microsoft made the key decision not to burden itself with the overhead of being backward-compatible with Windows Mobile.

The new approach is to make the user experience more convenient and reliable. There is also a new approach to applications development and control of apps after they're in the hands of users. This is all good, but it can be frustrating and confusing for Windows Mobile programmers.

If you have any preconceived notions from experience working with Microsoft's Windows Mobile in the past, forget them and read on.

Keep in mind, though, that Windows Phone 7 is a work in progress. Microsoft will be continuously improving it. If you're disappointed with a particular feature or capability, chances are, it'll be addressed eventually.

Windows Phone 7: A Single-Threaded Operating System

One of the big surprises many pundits have expressed about the Windows Phone 7 OS is that it's a single-threaded operating system. This means that it can run only one application at a time. Other smartphones, such as those based on Android, make a point of saying that they run multiple apps at once.

A Windows Phone simply pauses the application that isn't visible on-screen. The advantage of this is that it allows for minimizing the memory footprint by allowing only one application at a time to use memory. If you plan for this (which we recommend, by the way), the user won't be able to tell the difference.

The application you're writing will need to run on a single-threaded operating system. This is easy — all you need to do is make sure that your application can be paused. The power of the processor in the phone is entirely devoted to your application when it's running.

So, what if you want to receive word if something interesting happens? One solution is to keep your communication up and running. The problem is that you can't do anything else! (This is somewhat of an oversimplification, but let's go with it.) To give you communication over the network when another application is running, Microsoft offers a function called *push notification* to take care of it. With push notification, the device is always visible to the network, but it has to interact with only one application at a time, if there is any communication at all.

A push notification is a "piece of toast" that just pops up on the screen during another application. For example, a weather application isn't currently running, but an update in the weather occurs. The Microsoft-hosted server sends this information to the phone. At the top of the screen is a notification bar. If the bar is activated, the phone pauses the application being used, and the information from the weather app pops up on the screen.

Your application can take advantage of this function. For example, if your app provides sports scores, a change in score might prompt a push notification, sending this information to the phone. The user then can click on the notification and activate your app.

The Windows Phone development model

Applications that run on the new Windows Phone environment are *sandboxed,* which means that they can't interact with other applications other than through the defined APIs. This is different from Windows Mobile and some other smartphone environments that allow developers to write native applications.

Some would say that this is a step backward; some developers find that having to write code within a sandbox is limiting. However, Microsoft did not make this decision lightly. There are two primary reasons why Microsoft made this choice:

✓ **Microsoft found that even professionals writing for Windows Mobile were tempted to go places where they shouldn't, making the phone unstable.** Sandboxed applications prevent this from happening.

✓ **There is great value to be gained from encouraging nonprofessional developers, like many of the readers of this book.** Making application development easier opens up mobile applications development to the creativity of people whose long suit is not development. This is very powerful. The challenge is that nonprofessionals are prone to get in over their heads and mess with capabilities that they have no business messing with. A sandboxed environment helps make this less likely. This is important in the mobile environment. Microsoft tried its best to work with native applications with the Windows Phone Classic OSs with mixed success. Perhaps Microsoft will allow some capabilities outside the sandbox in later releases, but for now, accept this decision and enjoy the stability that it offers for the environment.

We describe push notification more fully in Chapter 15, but the main consideration is that apps that require intensive data communications aren't suitable for the Windows Phone 7 platform. Of course, you could make the case that they aren't suitable for *any* smartphone, but that's a problem for other platforms to manage when those apps suck the juice out of the battery and leave the user disappointed in the device's battery life.

Your App on the Windows Phone

Lots of application resources are available for you to use. To begin to put these in context, we start with the diagram in Figure 3-1, which presents a conceptual map of where your application lies on the Windows Phone.

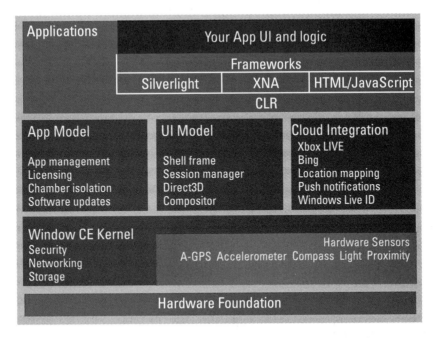

Figure 3-1: A map of the software model for Windows Phone 7.

There are four levels to this model. Starting at the bottom and working up:

⮑ **The hardware platform,** which for our purposes includes the processor, the GPU, the screen and digitizer, the hardware buttons, and the sensors

⮑ **Windows Phone 7 OS:**

- The kernel and a host of valuable libraries: Runtime, Resources, Globalization, Reflection, Location, Text, I/O, .NET, Diagnostics, Security, Threading, Collections, Component Model, Configuration, Service Model, and LINQ

  The idea behind the libraries is to offer programming shortcuts for regularly invoked application tools. For example, there is a box within the class libraries called LINQ, which stands for Language Integrated Queries. LINQ libraries are used when you create an app to perform queries. Instead of having to write your own tools for making queries, you learn how to use LINQ queries, and you're set.

- The APIs for the sensors

✔ **Three support systems:**

- The app model, which controls the management of the apps, including verifying that the device is properly licensed to run a given application and that it has the current release

- UI controls, which support your use of colors and fonts

- The cloud, which is another name for Internet computing

✔ **The frameworks,** which care whether the application is a web app, an XNA-based app, or a Silverlight-based app. Windows Phone 7 applications use the platforms of Microsoft Silverlight for most applications and XNA for games. These platforms allow you to create captivating applications that the consumer will love (and buy!). Part II covers everything you need to know about developer tools, including Silverlight.

✔ **Your app**

Your app is at the top of the pile, because this is what the user interacts with. Below it are all the application resources that you deem necessary and valuable for your app. You can ignore the rest of the resources. In fact, when you submit your application, part of the process is to tell the phone what resources you need and which you do not. In this way, the phone can save some battery power by not having all the app resources standing by.

Cloud Computing

The Windows Phone is built on the assumption that the device will be connected to the Internet the vast majority of the time. Basing an app on accessing data from the Internet is a reasonable approach. Until recently, writing a mobile app meant offering a stand-alone, isolated app that could access information only on the phone. With mobile OSs like the one on the Windows Phone, you can add a lot of value simply by reformatting a full PC screen onto the smaller phone screen. In most cases, you should add some value to information from the Internet.

Getting data from the cloud

Before downloading the tools to create an app (see Chapter 5), you need to decide which websites will be providing the information for your app. You can use one website or several websites. For example, a sport-score application could use just www.nfl.com, or it could use www.nba.com and www.nhl.com, too (as long as you have proper approval from the sites to access their data).

The mobile environment

If you're an experienced desktop programmer writing in the mobile environment for the first time, you need to keep in mind a couple key ways in which the mobile environment differs.

First, you need to pay attention to power management. Yes, ARM-based chips are more energy efficient than Intel-based chips, but the processor is not the only power user on the phone. At the top of the list is the Super AMOLED screen. It may seem like the user controls when the screen is in use and how fast the phone goes into sleep mode and blanks the screen. In fact, there are ways you can create screens that draw less power (each of these steps is small, but they add up):

✔ **Use white type on a black background.** Unlike previous cellphone screens where there is no difference in power usage, the less color coming off the screen, the less battery power is used.

✔ **Limit the animation of images.** Of course, it looks better to animate, but animation comes at a cost.

✔ **If your app uses the push function, set the default with a lower frequency.**

Also, don't forget the obvious: Mobile devices travel. This isn't a big surprise, but there are implications to this that are foreign to application development on a PC:

✔ **Phones get lost.** According to market research at In-Stat, over 98 percent of all people think they are better than average at keeping track of their cellular phone. Losing a plain old cellphone is frustrating, but losing a Windows Phone can be traumatic because the user loses all his personal information, too. Some people put security on their devices (for example, screensavers) to make it that much harder for thieves to access their data. Your app need to accept the way that screensavers work on the phone.

✔ **Phones are used in other countries.** Some PC developers are familiar with export restrictions on PCs. With Windows Phone application development, you need to consider what happens when the device is carried internationally.

Using social networks such as Facebook may be important to your application. Obtaining e-mail might be a feature. Posting pictures to the Internet may be needed. Your mobile app can use any or all of these data formats. Grabbing these data from the Internet, integrating them in some new way, and presenting the information creatively is easy. In fact, the Windows Phone offers you tools for doing this (see Chapter 10).

Counting the bars: Inconsistent connectivity

Users won't always have internet connectivity at every moment they want to use the phone. Phone users are rarely sitting in one location while using an app. Even if they are, the quality of coverage adjusts based upon the number of users on a network at any given moment. Although the phone supplements cellular data coverage with Wi-Fi service, by having both options available, there are places where the use of any radio is prohibited, such as some areas within a hospital or in airplanes that don't have Wi-Fi service.

The reality is that your app may have periods of time where there are no bars. If no data is available, your app shouldn't crash. Even better, the app should be able to gracefully handle the inevitable absence of coverage.

Application Model Rollout

When you're done with the programming, Visual Studio bundles the files up into a larger XAP file. (We will discuss this subject more on this starting in Chapter 8.) Then you submit the app to Microsoft, which tests it to certify that the app will actually run, doesn't violate laws, and doesn't include any malware (see Chapter 16). Assuming that your app is approved, it's available on the Windows Phone Marketplace, the only source for apps on the Windows Phone.

Apps can't be installed from the user's computer directly (called *side-loading*). They also can't be purchased from another digital storefront.

In addition, the phone will check back with the Windows Phone Marketplace each time the user launches the app. This makes sure that the license is valid and that no malware has slipped onto the phone.

When (not if) you develop a new version, this checking provides you the opportunity to alert users to updates. More on this in Chapter 20.

4

Doing the Legwork Before You Put Your Fingers to the Keyboard

In This Chapter

▶ Considering your app's capabilities

▶ Categorizing your app

▶ Storyboarding your app

▶ Evaluating the development environments

*W*hen you're thinking about developing an app, you may want to dive in head first — and we don't blame you! Application development can be challenging and thrilling, all at the same time. But before you get ahead of yourself, spend a little time thinking about what kind of app you want to write. You may already have an idea, but even so, it's wise to think about all your options.

After you've decided what your app will be, make like a filmmaker and storyboard your app: Sketch out (either by hand or on the computer) the various screens of your app. This kind of detail work is what will set your app apart from the crowd. Finally, familiarize yourself with the development environment so you know what to expect.

In this chapter, we cover all these subjects, helping you lay the foundation for the development of a successful app.

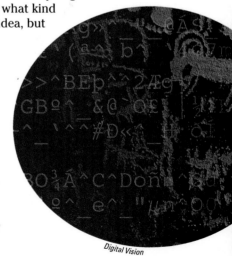

Digital Vision

Conceptualizing Your App

Before you start programming, you need to consider, and then define, the high-level capabilities of your app. Consider what information you want your app to have and how often you want the information to refresh.

Refreshing too often drains the battery and may be prohibited by Microsoft in the submission process.

Resist the temptation to put too much on a screen. An overload of information is worse than too little. You don't have to hire a user-interface expert, but presenting information in an attractive format on the screen is a large part of the value you provide.

Think about your potential market. Do you want to focus on a small group of people, such as helping users find the closest sushi restaurant? Or do you want to help a large group of people, such as helping users find the closest gas station?

Most developers start out wanting to serve as large an audience as possible. But it's often more profitable to serve a small market extremely well than a large market adequately.

If you're using a map application, do you want it to reorient each time the user turns? The Windows Phone is able to locate where it is, but the user has the option of making this information available to your app or blocking it.

Don't forget that your app may be used on three different screens: the PC, the phone, and the TV. You may just want to get the app on the market, but there is great value in supporting the "three-screen model." Thinking about all this now will pay great dividends later on.

These are just a few of the issues to consider. The main point is that every minute that you spend in planning and preparing pays dividends in terms of helping you avoid potential pitfalls down the road.

Considering App Categories

When it comes to developing a new app, you're limited only by your imagination. Here's how the Windows Phone Marketplace (`http://marketplace.windowsphone.com`) categorizes apps. Look over this list to get a sense of where your idea fits or to inspire you to come up with even more ideas:

✔ **Games:** This category in the Windows Phone Marketplace has the most apps — so many, in fact, that the Games category is subdivided as follows:

- **Action:** These games focus on challenges that rely on hand-eye coordination.

- **Classic:** Classic games include familiar video games, mostly from the 1970s and 1980s, that have been reformatted for the Windows Phone.

- **Board:** This category includes games of strategy, involving the movement of pieces based upon a set of rules.

- **Card & Casino:** These are chance and strategy games, involving decks of virtual cards, dice, or other gambling devices.

- **Education:** Educational games have the goal of imparting information in a fun way.

- **Family & Kids:** This category is for games with appeal to both children and parents.

- **Word & Puzzle:** As the title implies, these are games that involve words and puzzles.

- **Music:** Any games that involves music belong in this category.

- **Driving:** Driving games are a special type of action games.

- **Strategy:** While many games involve strategy to some degree, the games in this category are about pursuing a goal in a universe created by the author of the game.

- **Simulation:** Games in this category emulate some aspect of reality.

- **Sports:** These games emphasize some elements of the strategy of familiar competitive sports.

✔ **Entertainment:** The apps that fall into the Entertainment category aren't games, but they're still fun. They include trivia, horoscopes, and frivolous noisemaking apps.

✔ **News & Weather:** This category includes a variety of apps that allow the user to get just the news or weather that's most relevant to him, instead of what's available on the extended Start screen. The category is subdivided as follows:

- **News**

- **Weather**

- **Sports**

✔ **Productivity:** The apps in this category help the user be more productive. This category is subdivided as follows:

- **Time Management:** This includes calendars, reminders, alarms, and project tracking apps.

- **Money Management:** Money management apps are tools to calculate tips, monitor exchange rates, and track expenses.

- **Task Management:** These apps allow you to transfer paper-based "to do" lists to your phone.

✔ **Social Networks:** The apps in this category are related to social-networking sites. Here, you find apps that allow users to engage with Facebook, LinkedIn, Twitter, MySpace, and more.

✔ **Communication:** The Windows Phone comes with many communications applications, but the apps in this category enhance what comes with the phone. For example, you can find tools that automatically send a message if you're running late to a meeting or that text you if your kids leave a defined area.

✔ **Lifestyle:** The Lifestyle category is a catch-all for applications that involve recreation or special interests, like coin collecting or cooking. It's divided into the following subcategories:

- **Health & Fitness:** Apps in this category help the user track progress or provide information on health and/or fitness goals.

- **Recreation:** This category enhances the user's experience in recreational activities.

- **Photography:** The Windows Phone already comes with some very good apps for taking and categorizing photos, but the apps in this category let users get creative with editing and reformatting images.

- **Shopping:** For some people, shopping can be a source of recreation or a competitive sport. This is the category for them.

- **More:** This category includes anything that doesn't fit nicely into the other categories.

✔ **Music & Video:** The phone comes with the Zune music and video service, but nothing says you have to like it or even use it. This category includes apps that offer an alternative to Zune.

✔ **Maps & Search:** Many applications in this category tell you where you are and how to get where you want to go. Some apps are updated with current conditions like traffic and weather, and others are based upon static maps that use typical travel times. This category is subdivided as follows:

- **Maps:** These apps just show you where your selected destination is located on a map.

- **Local Search:** These apps use local knowledge of the area to show what you're seeking.

✔ **Travel:** This category includes apps that are useful for traveling — everything from currency converters to travel guides to mileage calculators to flight trackers.

✔ **Business Center:** This category is all about — you guessed it — business. It's divided into the following subcategories:

- **Inventory:** These apps tell you how much stuff you have.

- **Dashboards:** Dashboards visually present dynamically changing information patterned after the dashboard on your car. For example, you know where the speedometer and odometer are on your car's dashboard. A dashboard for a business can display up-to-the minute business results, such as daily sales results or stock prices.

- **Services:** This category includes the productivity tools relevant to a service business, such as schedules of available workers, order forms, and the screens needed to take credit card payments from customers.

- **CRM:** Customer records management (CRM) systems keep all customer files accessible in one place. Many CRM systems are primarily updated by inside salespeople and customer service agents, but mobile salespeople can access and enter data from their Windows Phone devices.

- **Documents:** Inevitably, mobile workers need documents that they didn't anticipate needing. Document apps give them access to the latest versions of the docs they need.

- **Manufacturing:** A great deal of manufacturing is automated, and these apps offer mobile workers access to this information from their phones.

- **Real Estate:** Real estate professionals use automation tools for selling, pricing, and inspecting homes. These apps keep real estate pros from having to travel back to the office to enter or access this information.

- **Time & Expense:** Company management and many professionals need to document and track their time for management reports and customer billing. Apps in this category help them track their hours and spending.

- **Unified Comms:** Some companies use packages that combine e-mail, instant messaging, Voice over Internet Protocol (VoIP) calling, and status monitoring tools to enhance business communications. Enabling such a package on a Windows Phone offers similar capabilities when the worker is not at her desk.

- **Data Collection:** The sole job of some workers is to collect data from the field, record it, and report it back to the office. When the information collected is sent immediately, the office can identify mistakes or unusual conditions right away. Businesses can collect the data and send it back to the office with the apps in this category.

- **Field Service:** Field service workers include mobile repairmen, delivery services, and installation technicians. The apps in this category can give them all the information they need as well as providing management back in the office their status and results.

- **Finance:** Financial professionals can leave the office and visit clients at their homes or offices while being able to access real-time information on stock prices and interest rates on their Windows Phone with the apps in this category.

- **Health Care:** Healthcare paperwork can be automated and moved to a Windows Phone with these apps. Healthcare workers also can access patient records and medical information at the site of the patient, rather than obliging the patient to go where it's convenient for the healthcare provider.

- **More:** Apps that don't fit in any of the other categories can be found here.

✔ **Reference:** The apps in the Reference category include a range of reference books, such as dictionaries and translation guides. Think of this like the reference section of your local library or bookstore.

✔ **Books:** Who needs an e-reader? You can read books on your Windows Phone. The Books category is subdivided as follows:

- **Readers:** These are the platforms for accessing electronic books.

- **Fiction:** This category includes novels and other works of fiction.

- **Non-Fiction:** This category is for reference books, biographies, histories, and other works of nonfiction.

✔ **Tools:** Some of the apps in this category are widgets that help with some fun and/or interesting capabilities. Others are more complicated and help you get more functionality from your phone. For example, some users may prefer an alarm clock that operates differently from the one that comes standard on your phone. The Tools category includes this kind of app.

Defining the Logical Flow of Your App

Effective apps have a natural and intuitive flow among the various screens. The idea is that you should be able to explain the logical flow of your app to a willing audience. If you can't, a novice user won't bother taking the time to figure out your app — there are too many other apps out there competing for the user's attention.

How much effort you have to put into the logical flow of your app depends on how complicated your app is. If all you want your app to do is provide the score from today's Major League Baseball games, the app may consist of only one screen with the scores. If your app is more complicated, you'll need to spend a bit more time thinking about how the user will move from one screen to another. In this case, consider *storyboarding* your app — sketching out how each screen will look and how the user will flow from one screen to the next. We cover storyboarding in this section.

In addition to figuring out how users will get from one screen to the next, you need to know what those screens will look like. You'll use the Metro user interface, the design standard user interface used on Windows Phone 7. In this section, we introduce you to Metro.

Storyboarding your app

No matter how simple your app will be, you should plan it out step by step. Prepare a screen layout for every logical step in the process, starting with the icon or "token" that will appear on the phone, the splash screen that a user will see during application launch, and the first screen that you present to the user for instructions.

From there, you need to plot out the logic of your application, using logic trees as needed. A *logic tree* (like the one shown in Figure 4-1) provides a visual representation of choices you can make and the resulting options and possible outcomes. The challenge is to make sure you have a template for every way that a user could logically progress in your application.

You may have been eating, sleeping, and breathing this app for months, but your users will be starting fresh, and you want them to be able to move through your app seamlessly.

Most professionals take great pains to create a formal process before starting coding. Even if your app is linear from one screen to the next, like a comic strip, you still need to plot out the screens.

The instant that you get into logical branches, you can easily make a mistake. A sample of a nonlinear logic flow is shown in Figure 4-2.

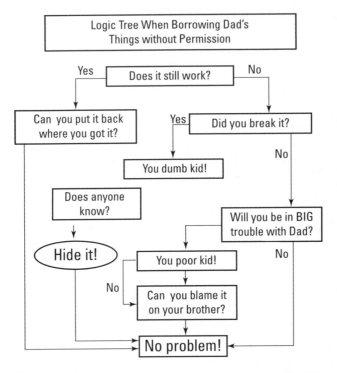

Figure 4-1: A logic tree can help you envision how users will move around in your app.

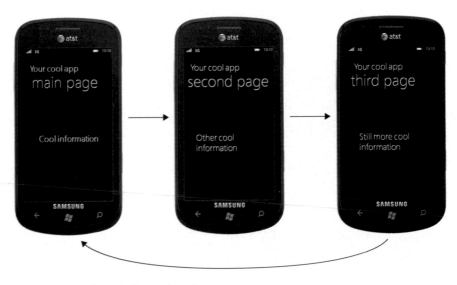

Figure 4-2: A nonlinear logic storyboard.

If you don't follow this discipline and mess up your logic when coding, you'll waste an immense amount of time correcting the problem. That's why professionals — who are very experienced in application logic — still use storyboarding tools. (Have we convinced you of the importance of storyboarding yet?)

Designing the screen layout: The Metro user interface

After you have the logical flow of your app (see the preceding section), you're ready to design the screen layout. You get to be creative in what information you put where, but there are guidelines that Microsoft strongly encourages you to use. These guidelines follow what Microsoft calls the Metro user interface (UI).

The Metro UI is the design standard user interface used on Windows Phone 7. Based on the Zune HD interface, it's clean, light, open, and fast. Instead of using 3D images, it uses motion and animation to create an experience that's different from that of other smartphones.

The source of the name Metro is that street signs in almost all countries are clean and simple, communicating a great deal of information efficiently. Even if you don't understand the language, you can usually figure out when you need to stop, and where parking lots, phones, and restrooms are located.

White type on a black background is standard (but users can select something different as part of their Theme settings). The Segoe font is the standard. You'll be fine if you simply follow the guidelines of Visual Studio — don't worry about distinguishing your app by having fancier (read: complicated) graphics.

The Metro UI has certain requirements to make it more usable on the phone:

✔ The objects must be at least 7mm in size and spaced by at least 2mm. The hit zone for this object may be larger — at least 9mm.

✔ Using the application content and gestures should imitate real life. For example, touching a picture will open it, and sliding a finger on it will pan to move it. There should be an immediate reaction in your app to user actions such as a tilting the phone.

✔ The user interface should have a unique and exciting feel by translating touch gestures (tap, double tap, pan, touch and hold, pinch, stretch, and flick) into a colorful experience.

These requirements are easily met using Silverlight.

A PDF from Microsoft, UI Design and Interaction Guide for Windows Phone 7 (available at http://go.microsoft.com/fwlink/?LinkID=183218), gives you all the nitty-gritty details on fonts, text size, and positioning. An even quicker tutorial is playing with a Windows Phone for a few minutes. All the basic screens are built with the Metro UI. √

Understanding the Processing Environment on the Windows Phone

In this section, we set the stage for understanding the environment in which your apps will be operating. This information is important for you to know in order to appreciate the capabilities (and some of the limitations) you'll face when you start coding.

If you've worked with Windows Phone Classic operating systems, you'll notice that the new Windows Phone is different.

Evaluating development environments

There are two application environments on the Windows Phone: Silverlight and XNA. As a general rule, Silverlight is primarily intended for apps, whereas XNA has its origins on the Xbox, so it's intended for games. However, no one is stopping you from writing a game in Silverlight or an app on XNA. In this section, we provide more information on these environments.

Hi-yo, Silverlight!

The Windows Phone 7 applications are based on a system initially designed to make websites exciting and visually bold in Internet Explorer. Some people like to call this system "Microsoft's Java," but the official name is Silverlight.

Silverlight is an incredibly easy-to-use programming tool. It makes writing an app in the Metro UI a breeze. Drop-down menus, color palettes, and animations are built in. (For much more information on Silverlight and why it's such a great tool, turn to Chapter 7. For even *more* info on Silverlight, check out *Microsoft Silverlight 4 For Dummies,* by Mahesh Krishnan and Philip Beadle [published by Wiley].)

XNA to the rescue

XNA is the language used for programming Xbox. Your Windows Phone runs applications that are written in XNA. The good news is that you can write XNA applications with the free tools that you download (see Chapter 5).

Foreground or background processing

When your app is running in a sandbox, it'll be functioning in an isolated area with no ability to affect other sandboxes. Your app will operate on top most of the time. If there is a phone call, the operating system will automatically move the application into the background.

To put it simply, when an app is visible on the screen, it's active and can take input. Conversely, if you can't see the app, it's either suspended or closed. You need to make sure that this can happen without your app blowing up. Think about it like pausing a DVD or turning off the machine.

The first bit of bad news is that this book does not go into programming with XNA. In practice, you can write functional user apps in XNA. You also can write games that run in Silverlight. To keep things in this book accessible, we made the decision to focus on programming only in Silverlight.

However, if you're determined to write for the Xbox, most of this book covers the process for working with the Windows Phone. This information applies whether you're running in Silverlight or XNA.

If you go the XNA way, remember that the Windows Phone 7 screen is a different resolution from television screens. You'll need to jigger your storyboard to accommodate TV screens.

Building authorized code into your apps

Creating your own code from scratch can be fun and rewarding — and a total waste of time. Don't reinvent the wheel for standard capabilities.

Getting code from other people

When you've decided what app you want to write, you may be able to find and use someone else's code. The programming community is often very generous — many programmers take great pride in offering their development to peers. The best source of code for the Windows Phone is the Microsoft Developer Portal (see Chapter 6).

Don't just copy some code, slap your name on it, and put it on the Marketplace. Not only is that uncool, but also, it probably violates the terms that you agreed to when you downloaded the person's work.

When using code written by others, be sure to *understand,* not just agree to, the terms and conditions. When you do take some code and incorporate it into your app, you're expected to personalize it and otherwise add some value before you put it in the Marketplace.

Using what's already on the phone

When planning the app you want to write, you need to know what comes installed on the phone. At the very least, this information is important so you can offer something better. Here's a list of capabilities that are on all Windows Phones:

- **Phone tasks:** Windows Phone 7 won't let you create a phone dialer. However, you can send your user to the existing dialer. If you have a message that should be communicated by a direct phone call, you can give your user the option to have the phone make a call. Your application will be paused during the phone call.

- **Launchers:** Your app can launch any of the tasks on the phone. The Navigator, messaging, and the tasks in the People hub are examples of things that could add a great deal to your app. Feel free to use these apps that are already on the phone. Why use MapQuest when the built-in Navigator inside Bing is already there?

- **E-mail:** E-mail is an important part of all our lives (just ask the U.S. Postal Service). Using e-mail with your app will make it more attractive. You can create an app that includes sending, receiving, or presenting e-mails on the phone.

Part II
Assembling the Tools You Need as a Developer

The 5th Wave   By Rich Tennant

RICHTENNANT

"He seemed nice, but I could never connect with someone who had a ring tone like his."

efore writing an application, you need to prepare, not only mentally but also in terms of developing a support system that will help you tackle the detailed programming issues that you may face. The first step is to prepare your PC by downloading the software tools that are available to help you create apps. Microsoft offers valuable help beyond what we offer in this book, and in this part, we tell you how to access that help. Finally, we introduce you to Silverlight, the runtime environment we use in this book for application development.

Photo credits: PhotoDisc/Getty Images (top, middle, bottom)

5

Downloading the Tools You Need

. . . .

. . . .

*M*icrosoft has made writing apps cheap and easy, with (almost) instant and constant gratification. The tool acquisition process starts off with installing the programming tools that you need if they aren't already on your PC. The install program detects what's currently installed on your computer and customizes the installation.

After you're done downloading the tools and letting them run through their installation and configuration process, you can design, code, and complete your app. Then your app must be debugged, validated by Microsoft, and finally deployed. In other words, it's sent to the Marketplace so you can reap the rewards (read: "money").

We start this chapter by telling you how to get a Windows Live ID. Then we walk you through the tool installation process. Finally, we offer a brief introduction to Visual Studio and the tools that you use to begin programming.

PhotoDisc/Getty Images

Getting a Windows Live ID

Before you can do anything, you must have a Windows Live ID. You already have a Windows Live ID if:

✔ You have an e-mail account from Microsoft, ending in `msn.com`, `hotmail.com`, or `live.com`.

✔ You have an earlier version of the Windows Phone, formerly known as Windows Mobile, and have access to the Windows Marketplace.

✔ You signed up for one of the following services from Microsoft:

  • Microsoft Instant Messaging Service

  • Windows Live Calendar

  • Windows Live Contacts

  • Windows Live Essentials

  • Windows Live Profile

  • Windows Live SkyDrive

  • Windows Live Writer

  • Windows Movie Maker

  • Windows Photo Gallery

  • Xbox Live Service

  • Zune

✔ You signed up for an earlier version of the Windows Live ID when it was called Microsoft Wallet, Microsoft Passport, or .NET Passport.

If you don't already have a Windows Live ID, you can get one at `http://login.live.com`.

Knowing Which Tools You Need

The two main tools you'll use for developing Windows Phone 7 apps are the following:

✔ **Visual Studio 2010 for Windows Phone 7:** Visual Studio allows you to create attractive screens for your app and takes you through the development process.

✔ **Windows Phone Emulator:** The Windows Phone Emulator allows you to test your application extensively before it hits the Marketplace.

When you're downloading the Windows Phone Developer Tools, you may see a list of other applications that you'll download at the same time, most of which are used behind the scenes. For example, if you don't already have Microsoft .NET Framework, Microsoft Visual Studio C++, and some other utilities, the Microsoft website will detect this and have you download and install them on your PC. Don't be concerned with these tools — just download the tools the Microsoft site tells you to download, and you'll be fine.

Windows Phone Developer Tools are available in English, French, Italian, German, and Spanish.

In addition to needing these tools, you need a fairly new computer. Even a system bought a couple years ago is sluggish when running these mammoths. (Trust us — we know from firsthand experience.) You need plenty of memory (at least 2 GB, but ideally 6 GB or more), processing power (at least 1 GHz, but preferable a quad-core at 1.5 GHz or more), and storage space (at least 3 GB, but preferably more) to accommodate them.

Downloading the Free Tools

Using the PC you plan to use for development, go to the App Hub (`http://create.msdn.com`). From there, follow these steps:

1. **Click the "Download the free tools" link in the upper-left corner (see Figure 5-1).**

Figure 5-1: The App Hub home page.

This brings up the screen shown in Figure 5-2. Toward the bottom are the links to begin downloading the tools you need.

2. **Click the link that says, "Download and install the Windows Phone Developer Tools."**

   Clicking that link brings up the familiar application download screen. (You don't need to download the release notes.) The smart loader checks your machine and starts downloading only what you need.

3. **Click the link that says, "Download and install the Windows Phone Developer Tools January 2011 Update."**

   Again, you'll see a familiar download screen.

4. **Go get a drink.**

   The January 2011 Update takes a while to install. Be patient.

5. **Click the link that says, "Download and install the Windows Phone Developer Tools Fix."**

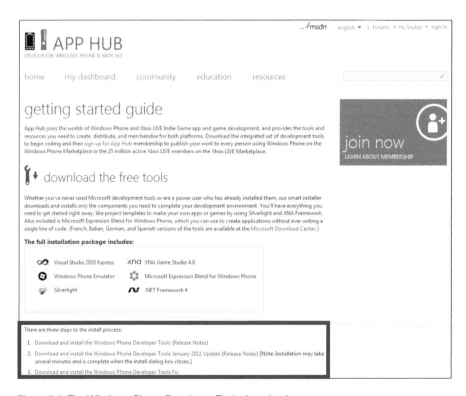

Figure 5-2: The Windows Phone Developer Tools download screen.

After you've followed these steps, you have every tool that you need to build, validate, and publish your app. If you already have Visual Studio 2010 Professional, the Windows Phone Emulator is the only tool that will be installed. If you have any previous editions of Visual Studio, XNA Game Studio, or Windows Mobile 6, more tools will be installed.

In the following sections, we fill you in on Visual Studio Express 2010 and the Windows Phone Emulator, your two main tools.

Introducing Visual Studio Express 2010

After you've downloaded Visual Studio Express 2010, your PC will expect you to open Visual Studio to configure it on your PC. Go ahead and satisfy your PC: Click the new desktop icon (shown in Figure 5-3). You should see something similar to Figure 5-4.

Figure 5-3: Microsoft's Visual Studio Express 2010 desktop icon.

From this screen, you can create a new project or open an existing project. Because this is the first time you've used the software, open some of the application templates that come with Visual Studio, and look around. You can find these beneath the options to create a new project or open an existing project.

Click one of these templates. For purposes of illustration, we clicked the PanoramaPivotControls template to give you a sense of what an open project looks like (see Figure 5-5). This screen displays a lot of information. You'll want to be working on a high-resolution monitor to give yourself some working room.

Figure 5-4: A Visual Studio Express 2010 sample screen.

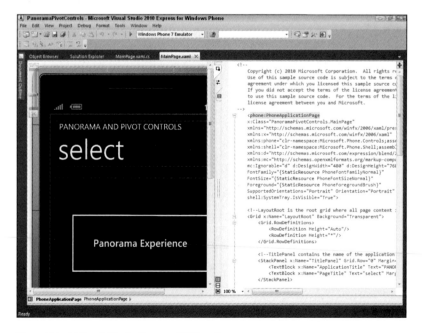

Figure 5-5: A Visual Studio Express 2010 main page screen.

When you're ready to start programming, Visual Studio is a concrete foundation that you can build on. There are simple drag-and-drop options that are written in XAML. It provides a rich user interface and animation. You can easily go back and forth between the different "views" of the app in development, giving you simultaneous access to the screen layout, the underlying code, and other development tools. We cover the "views" in Parts III and IV, but the idea is to make it simple for you to jump quickly to the programming element that allows you to be most productive at any given moment.

Windows Phone Emulator: Your New Best Friend

The Windows Phone Emulator is a high-fidelity and performance-virtualization environment. In other words, it has great sound and acts just like a phone. You can't make a call on it, but you can push buttons, use the touch screen (with your mouse), and simulate your app. The Windows Phone Emulator gives you the chance to see how your app executes and debug your app before submitting it to the Marketplace.

Starting the emulator

Now for the hard part. To start the emulator, you need to press — drum roll, please — F5. That's it. It should look like what you see in Figure 5-6.

Figure 5-6: A Windows Phone Emulator sample screen.

Do you even need a phone?

Yes, eventually, you do need a phone. About 80 percent of a phone app's debugging can be done on the emulator, but the gold standard is running it on a phone. Side-loading is possible with Windows Phone 7, but it's highly restricted.

You can only install app releases directly from your PC for final testing. So, be sure that you're ready when you start testing. Other than this, Windows Phone Marketplace is the only way to get the app to a phone.

The emulator will load the program you currently have open in Visual Studio.

What the emulator can do

The emulator has a real phone skin — the same buttons as a phone. You'll see a Back button, a Start button, and a Search button. When you left-click a button, it's like tapping a soft key on the screen or pressing a button. You can't pan or zoom because there is no equivalent for multitouch with a mouse (unless you have a multitouch computer screen). You can scroll the screen around by pressing the left mouse key to simulate a press and hold.

In addition, there is GPS simulation, so if your app needs the user's location, it will work. Orientation support means that if your user turns a corner, the map will turn as well.

Pest control: The debugger

In order to work out problems with program logic, you can use the debugger. It provides breakpoints by function, line, and conditionally. Exception handling is provided with dialog boxes and recommendations.

Some of the other processes that take place are cell stack walking, expression evaluation, source code stepping, and variable watch window. All this means is that if you mess up, there's a good chance that the debugger will help you fix the problem.

6

Building Your Mojo by Accessing the Microsoft Developer Portal

In This Chapter

▶ Using the App Hub

▶ Accessing the available tools on the Microsoft Software Developer Network

▶ Getting the most out the Windows Phone Developer Blog

So, you have the tools on your PC to write applications (see Chapter 5). Now what? You're ready to start programming! But before you dive in, we introduce you to the App Hub, a user-friendly site that Microsoft has developed to help nonprofessional developers. Then we introduce the Microsoft Software Developer Network (MSDN) website, which is set up for pros — it has more information in more formats than the App Hub, but it isn't as easy to navigate.

Note: We can't give you every tip, technique, and API that exists within the Windows Phone 7 environment. That's more information than this book can hold. Instead, we get you comfortable with the basics, give you context, and then point you to more detailed online resources in case you need more information.

Ryan McVay/PhotoDisc/Getty Images

Introducing the App Hub

If you've already downloaded the tools in Chapter 5, you've been to the App Hub (http://create.msdn.com), shown in Figure 6-1.

Figure 6-1: The App Hub home page.

Across the top, you see five links:

- ✔ **Home:** This just takes you back to the home page of the website.

- ✔ **My Dashboard:** The shows you important status information, including your sales volumes and status of submitted apps.

- ✔ **Community:** The Community link takes you to the blogs and FAQs of the application development community. You can save yourself valuable time by interacting with other Windows Phone 7 application developers as well as the Microsoft app development support team. The community also benefits when you ask questions.

- ✔ **Education:** Microsoft offers more in-depth training on many topics. This link takes you to your options.

- ✔ **Resources:** This link takes you to the other tools that Microsoft offers, including free downloads and offerings from Microsoft partners.

In the following sections, we pay particular attention to the Education and Community sections of the site.

Education

When you hover your mouse over the Education link, a list of options appears:

- ✓ **Education Catalog:** This is a list of the webcasts, code samples, and articles available for you to enhance your knowledge of app development in the Windows Phone 7 environment.

- ✓ **App Development:** This takes you to short presentations that walk you through some application development basics. These are a good complement to Parts III and IV of this book.

- ✓ **Game Development:** This option is targeted primarily to Xbox game developers who want to revise the games they've developed for Xbox for use on the Windows Phone.

- ✓ **Library Documentation:** This is a virtual card catalog of all Windows Phone 7 reference books available from Microsoft. This is a good place to go when you're looking for more detailed information.

- ✓ **Porting Guidance:** This option is for mobile app programmers who have written apps for other mobile platforms, like iOS or Android, and want help in converting these apps for use on the Windows Phone.

- ✓ **Developer Talks:** Microsoft arranges webinars on development topics once every month or so. You can learn about upcoming talks from this tab.

In the following sections, we home in on the Education Catalog and the Library Documentation.

Education Catalog

When you click the Education Catalog option, you see something like Figure 6-2. The site includes numerous options that are designed to help you with your programming, categorized as follows:

- ✓ **Articles:** Articles present information as text and images. Often, the articles reference other relevant articles. (See Figure 6-3 for typical results of an articles search.)

- ✓ **Code samples:** Code samples are offered to you under a permissive license where you use the code within another application. Typically, you download a zip file to get access to the code sample. (See Figure 6-4 for typical results of a code sample search.)

You must modify the code. It's counter to the terms of the permissive license to take code samples and use them unmodified. Plus, it's just not cool. You want to be original and do something that no one else has done. Combining two sets of code in a new way can be quick and easy, and it may address a need that no one else has addressed before.

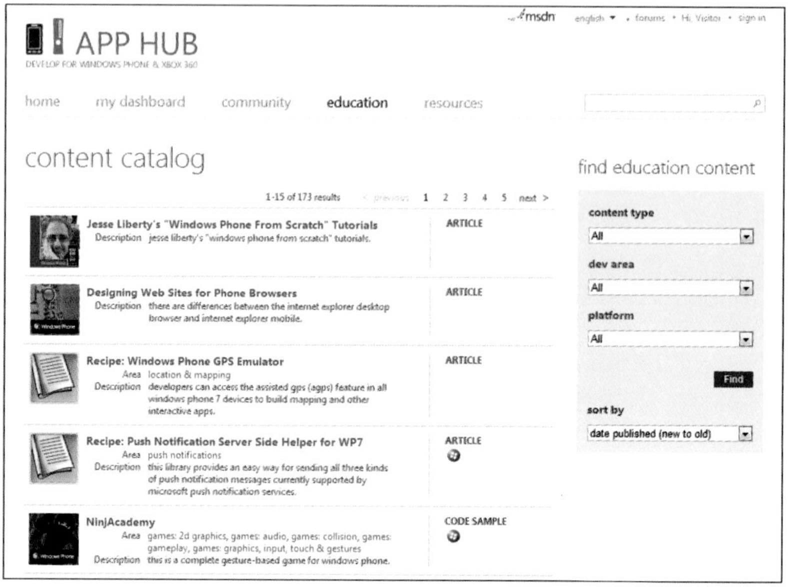

Figure 6-2: The Education Catalog screen of the App Hub.

Figure 6-3: Search results for articles.

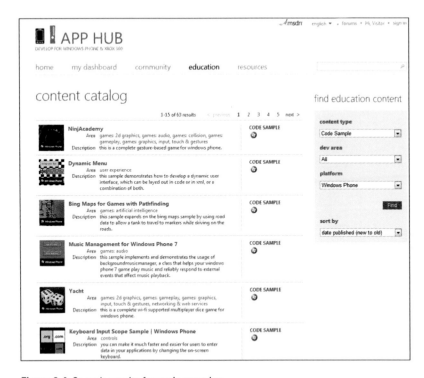

Figure 6-4: Search results for code samples.

If you're having trouble coming up with an idea for a novel app, look over the code samples. Something may jump out at you.

✔ **Tools:** The Tools category is a catch-all for helpful things. As you can see in Figure 6-5, there are sound files and performance monitoring tools. Check back from time to time to see what tools have been added to help your app run faster, make you more productive, or make your app more attractive to new customers.

✔ **Tutorials:** Tutorials help you learn more about a particular topic. In general, you download a zip file and watch or listen to the presentation at your convenience. Most are about 15 minutes long, and the quality varies along with the style and content.

To help you narrow your search, the Education Catalog categorizes the items into 27 development areas. Some of the development areas may not have any content yet, but the catalog is updated continuously, so be sure to check back.

Library Documentation

When you click the Library Documentation option under Education, you see something like Figure 6-6.

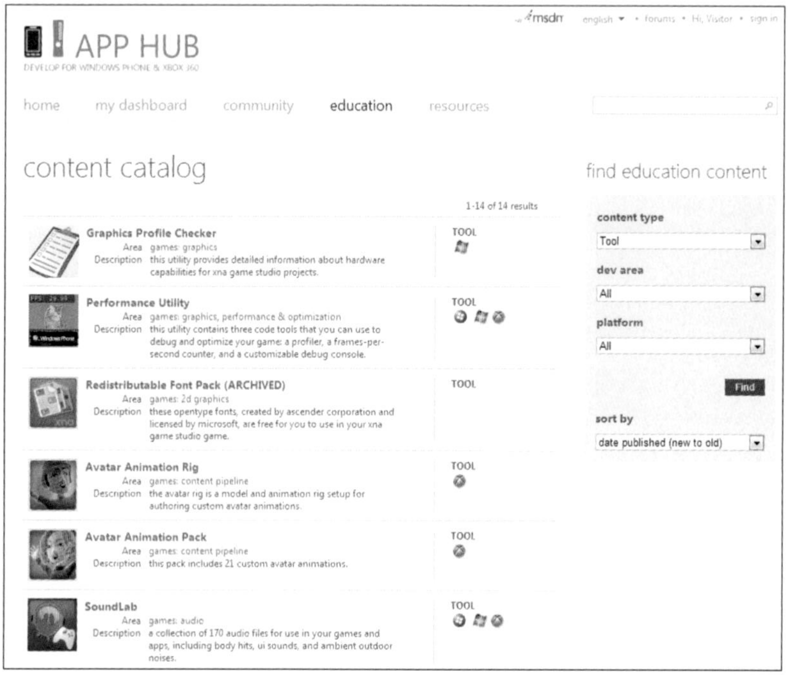

Figure 6-5: Search results for tools.

Click a link that looks interesting, and you'll be taken to a page on the MSDN site where that article appears. For example, if you were to click the link for "Windows Phone Development," you would see Figure 6-7. We cover the MSDN site later in this chapter.

Community

As you continue your adventure of developing applications for Windows Phone 7, you may find it helpful to know that there are other developers out there with the same kinds of questions you have. To support you, Microsoft offers a community where you can ask questions of experts. Just hover your mouse over the Community link at the App Hub (`http://create.msdn.com`), and click anything that looks interesting. Figure 6-8 shows the Community Resources page.

> Many Microsoft experts write blogs that you can search for more information. Each expert's area of expertise is listed by his name. To best use the experts' time and talent, check out the Windows Phone Developer Blog (`http://windowsteamblog.com/windows_phone/b/wpdev`), which is a combination of multiple blogs, so you can see which expert is most likely to meet your needs.

Figure 6-6: The Library Documentation screen of the App Hub.

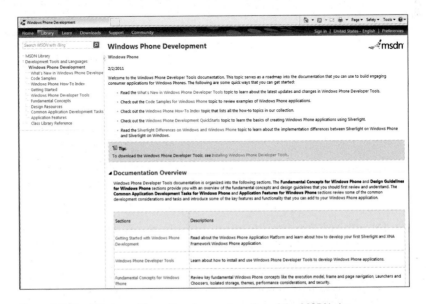

Figure 6-7: The Windows Phone Development section of the MSDN site.

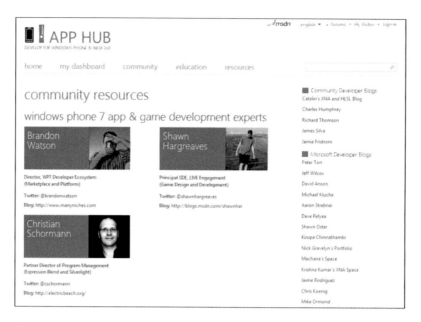

Figure 6-8: The Community Resources page.

Finding Your Way around the MSDN Windows Phone Developer Site

The information in the App Hub (see the previous section) is meant to be useful and accessible to nonprofessional developers. On the other hand, the information on the Microsoft Software Developer Network (MSDN) is for professionals — but that doesn't mean you can't take advantage of what it has to offer.

To get started, go to the MSDN site at `http://msdn.microsoft.com` (see Figure 6-9). Click the Phone link. You see the screen shown in Figure 6-10. This page offers many introductory videos and tutorials for Windows Phone development. It may be a matter of personal preference, but we think that the App Hub presents the same information more directly.

More valuable on the MSDN site are the links on the MSDN home page:

- ✔ **Home:** This just takes you back to the home page of the website.
- ✔ **Library:** The MSDN Library contains all the articles that relate to Microsoft development. Figure 6-11 highlights the section of the MSDN Library that covers Windows Phone development.

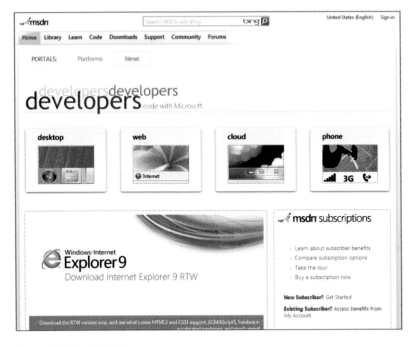

Figure 6-9: The MSDN home page.

Figure 6-10: The MSDN home page for Windows Phone.

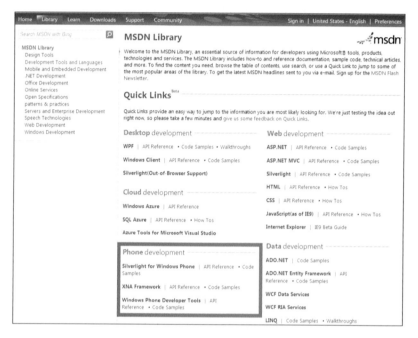

Figure 6-11: The MSDN Library.

These links take you to the same articles shown in Figure 6-6, earlier in this chapter; how you arrive at this information is your choice.

✔ **Learn:** The Learn link takes you to a range of topics (shown in Figure 6-12). Several options for learning are available on this page. On the right side of the screen are links to Microsoft Learning Resources. You can click these to learn about a particular product or to learn programming in general.

The most valuable lessons for our purposes are the videos in the "'How Do I' Videos by Subject" section. Figure 6-13 highlights the Windows Phone option. When you click the Windows Phone link, you see a long list of videos (see Figure 6-14). Spend some time exploring the videos to learn more about developing for Windows Phone 7.

✔ **Code:** When you click the Code link, you see a page with donated code samples. However, there are only a few samples on this page for Windows Phone (and there are dozens available on the App Hub). Why such a big difference? We can't explain it. Just remember that if you want code samples, you're better off going to the App Hub as of this writing. This may change, of course, so looking at both resources when you need something specific is always a good idea.

Figure 6-12: The MSDN Learn page.

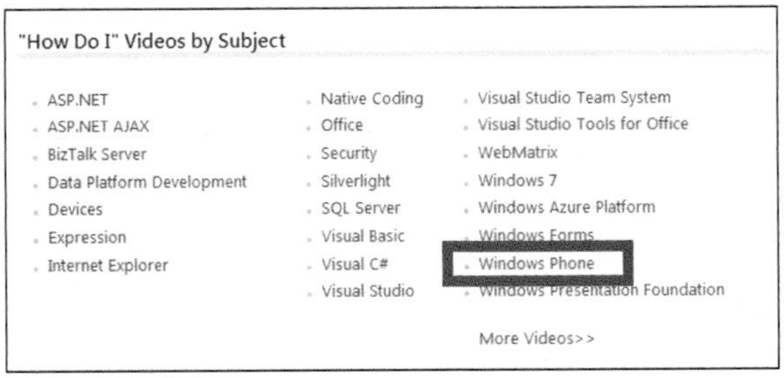

Figure 6-13: The MSDN "How Do I" Videos section.

✔ **Downloads:** Go ahead and skip this section. You've already downloaded everything you need (see Chapter 5).

✔ **Support:** Again, everything you want and need for support is in the App Hub.

✔ **Community:** One more time, skip it. If you want to interact with a community, stick with the App Hub.

✔ **Forums:** At this last link, Forums, you find older forums on two very important subjects: Windows Marketplace for Mobile and Windows Phone 7. To make things confusing, they moved new questions to the App Hub. Still, there is a wonderful archive of valuable information here. If you're struggling with a problem and you're too shy to ask on the new forum, this is a place to look for advice.

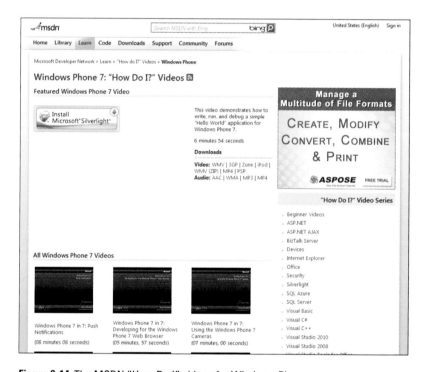

Figure 6-14: The MSDN "How Do I" videos for Windows Phone.

Monitoring the Windows Phone Developer Blog

Everything official on Windows Phone development is either on the App Hub (`http://create.msdn.com`) or on the MSDN site (`http://msdn.microsoft.com`). But the best place to find the most recent information on Windows Phone development topics is the Windows Phone Developer Blog (`http://windowsteamblog.com/windows_phone/b/wpdev`).

The blog is the best way to get the inside scoop on Windows Phone 7 development. All the news and announcements are here. Many of the blog entries start here and end up as articles that you can eventually search on the App Hub and the MSDN site.

7

Finding Your Direction with Silverlight

In This Chapter

▶ Introducing Silverlight and seeing how it's relevant for Windows Phone 7

▶ Exploring XAML

▶ Animating your apps

▶ Working with data in your apps

Silverlight is a technology that helps developers build immersive web applications for PCs. Microsoft chose Silverlight to be one of the runtimes on Windows Phone 7. Animations add the "wow" factor to your applications, and Silverlight provides developers the ability to create various kinds of animations with ease.

In this chapter, we introduce you to Silverlight and explain how it works in Windows Phone 7, as well as present the basics on creating animations in code. Then we show you how to use XAML (Extensible Application Markup Language) to create Silverlight applications for Windows Phone 7 so that you can submit applications for inclusion in the Windows Marketplace as we discuss in Chapter 16. Finally, we show you how to access data from within your Silverlight application.

PhotoDisc, Inc.

Understanding What Silverlight Is All About

Silverlight originated as companion technology of Windows Presentation Foundation (WPF). WPF was released with .NET Framework 3.0 and was meant to be used as the technology for building Windows-based desktop applications.

The .NET Framework is hard-core stuff for serious programmers. We'll keep it simple for this book, but it's good to know the power is there when you become more proficient.

Silverlight is meant to be a cross-platform and cross-browser plug-in that installs itself when someone visits a website built with Silverlight for the first time. If the user's security software is picky, the user may be asked to download Silverlight. After the user has downloaded Silverlight, subsequent visits to the same website or other sites built with Silverlight don't require the installation of the plug-in.

The history of Silverlight

The first version of Silverlight, originally named WPF/e (short for WPF/everywhere) was released in September 2007. However, the name WPF/e did not trip off the tongue lightly. Hence, it was renamed Silverlight.

Silverlight was targeted for enterprises planning to deliver a very sleek and immersive user experience through their websites. The first release of Silverlight had several limitations, and developers didn't flock to it, even though it had the new name. For example, the first version of Silverlight didn't include support for using the .NET Framework.

Silverlight 1.1 (later updated to version 2.0), announced in 2007, provided developers a version of the .NET Framework. Silverlight applications could be built with any .NET language, such as C# and Visual Basic .NET. Adoption by developers started to grow.

Silverlight 3, announced in September 2008, extended the features available for developers and allowed broadcasters to use smooth streaming of full high-definition video.

Microsoft continued adding features, and Silverlight 4 was released in April 2010. This release added webcam, microphone, and printing support, as well as a rich set of controls. Silverlight continued to gain popularity as the

platform on which to build and deliver rich user interfaces and streaming media.

Microsoft regularly publishes links to websites that use Silverlight in their core design. To get a sense of the capabilities of Silverlight on the web, a collection of sites is available at `www.silverlight.net/showcase`, including the following:

- **Diver2 (`www.farseergames.com/divergame2`)**: A simple but addictive game built with Silverlight

- **Microsoft Art & Technology (`www.microsoft.com/click/artandtechnology`)**: Microsoft's web portal showcasing next-generation web technologies

- **Shidonni (`www.shidonni.com`)**: A popular kids' site built with Silverlight and ASP. NET

- **Silverlight Samples (`www.silverlight.net/community/samples/silverlight-samples`)**: A collection of community-contributed samples of Silverlight applications and controls

- **SmoothHD (`www.smoothhd.com`)**: A website that hosts a collection of movie trailers and other media in high definition and uses Silverlight for streaming the media

Check out *Microsoft Silverlight 4 For Dummies,* by Mahesh Krishnan and Philip Beadle (Wiley), to learn more about Microsoft Silverlight. Tell 'em Bill and Indy sent you.

Silverlight's origin as a web animation tool

Animations in a website are used to add appeal to the rather plain look and feel of an ordinary website. When the GIF image format was introduced with support for animations, website developers started using animated GIF images in their websites. GIF images are perfect for creating simple animations. In order to create complex animations and introduce interactivity in a website, animated GIF images are not sufficient.

Microsoft Silverlight was initially introduced to provide streaming video in websites. It was enhanced in later releases as the alternative technology to Adobe Flash. Silverlight allows you to enhance existing websites built with HTML, CSS, and JavaScript by adding Silverlight content in a region of the website. You also may build a Silverlight-only website with some fancy content.

One of the simplest ways to enhance an existing website with Silverlight is to add a Silverlight menu to navigate through various pages. Go to `http://gallery.expression.microsoft.com/silverlightnav` and hover over the menu items to see the Silverlight animation in action. Figure 7-1 shows a simple menu built for a website with Silverlight.

Figure 7-1: A simple Silverlight menu control.

Silverlight has been used to create online games that can be played with any browser. Silverlight games use a mix of animations, media, and interactivity with the player for an engaging experience.

After the first use of a Silverlight application, games available online don't require installation of software on the player's computer, so they're very popular. You can view a good collection of games built with Silverlight at www.silverlightgames.org.

How Silverlight works on a phone

When Microsoft announced Windows Phone, Silverlight was selected as the platform for application development. This is a big incentive for existing Silverlight developers — their current skills could form the basis of learning how to build applications for Windows Phone 7.

Silverlight on Windows Phone 7 is available as a subset of the full Silverlight feature set with some additional features targeted for the phone.

If you're interesting in learning about the differences in Silverlight for Windows Phone 7 and full Silverlight, look at the list at http://msdn. microsoft.com/en-us/library/ff426930.

The Windows Phone 7 operating system is a "compact" version of the .NET Framework, popularly known as .NET Compact Framework. Silverlight for Windows Phone 7 runs on the .NET Compact Framework and supports XAML and code written for the .NET Framework. In addition to the main capabilities of Silverlight, such as graphics, animation, and media, the following Windows Phone 7–specific features are available:

- ✔ **Integration with phone features:** Developers can build applications that send text messages, initiate a phone call, and integrate with the Pictures hub and Music + Videos hub. In addition, the microphone and camera can be used as input devices to capture sound and images, and can be manipulated with Silverlight.

- ✔ **Multitouch:** Silverlight applications support the multitouch capabilities of the screen and GPU to provide pinch-to-zoom, rotate, and other transformations in an image-viewer application.

- ✔ **Location awareness:** Windows Phone 7 allows applications to add location-aware features, meaning that an application can use the GPS in your phone to realize where in the world you are at this moment.

- ✔ **Accelerometer:** The accelerometer in Windows Phone 7 provides motion-sensing features such as change in orientation and the speed at which the device is moving. (An accelerometer is rarely useful on a desktop PC unless you live on a fault line, so it isn't a standard capability.)

- ✔ **Push notifications:** Windows Phone 7 applications integrate push notifications, which allow you to communicate with your users even when your application isn't actively running.

Zeroing In on XAML

Website developers are familiar with HyperText Markup Language (HTML), the language used to create websites. Many, if not most, websites contain text, graphics, and embedded media such as video and audio. HTML provides developers a simple way to rapidly design and build websites. Tags are used to incorporate HTML elements, such as paragraphs of text and images, into a document. When a user's browser accesses the document, it interprets these elements and displays the content as expected.

Similarly, Silverlight applications use the Extensible Application Markup Language (XAML; pronounced *zah*-mel). With XAML, you can create a simple application without writing a single line of code! Silverlight ships with a nice set of controls that can be added to your application using XAML tags only.

However, XAML is not sufficient to create a real-world application. With XAML, you can't create objects or define events for common actions, such as clicking a button on a page. Silverlight applications consist of a combination of XAML and code written in C# or Visual Basic. XAML is used to define the screen layout of the application, and the code is used to manage the events of buttons, text boxes, and so on. XAML enables Silverlight application developers and user-interface designers to work together on the same application. Silverlight application developers create the basic user interface, which is then improved by the experts in graphic design to make the site more attractive. The graphics people often use Expression Blend.

Expression Blend is a part of the Expression suite of products that are aimed at graphic artists and professionals, but not necessarily beginners. Expression Blend is a useful tool to generate and edit XAML for Silverlight and WPF applications. You can read more about Expression Blend at `www.microsoft.com/expression/products/blend_overview.aspx`. Expression Blend for Windows Phone is shipped with the Windows Phone Developer Tools. You can explore Expression Blend for Windows Phone at `www.microsoft.com/expression/windowsphone/Default.aspx`. (To be clear, you do not need to learn how to use Expression Blend to write your app.)

Developers continue to work on the application, with code written in C# or Visual Basic .NET. Parts of a Silverlight application — such as accessing data from local storage or a remote data store, parsing XML, and playing media — are developed with code.

Because XAML is based on XML, it must be well formed and adhere to rules that apply to XML, such as white spaces, case sensitivity, matching tags, and so on. XAML is primarily used to declare controls and define animations. A Silverlight page is the fundamental building block of an application.

Here is some XAML that declares a button on a page:

```
<Page
  xmlns="http://schemas.microsoft.com/winfx/2006/xaml/presentation"
  xmlns:x="http://schemas.microsoft.com/winfx/2006/xaml">
  <Grid>
    <Button Width="120" Height="40">"Hello, World!"</Button>
  </Grid>
</Page>
```

Kaxaml (www.kaxaml.com) is a free tool that you can use to create simple Silverlight applications without writing any code. It complements the tools that you download from the Microsoft site (see Chapter 5). To get a feel for XAML, start Kaxaml and create a new Silverlight page (choose File⇨New Silverlight Tab, or press Ctrl + L). You'll find that Kaxaml has created the XAML markup where you can add your own user-interface items, such as buttons. Add the following XAML between the `<Grid>` `</Grid>` markup:

```
<Button Width="120" Height="40">"Hello, World!"</Button>
```

You'll find the Silverlight page with a button (see Figure 7-2). This example gives you a glimpse of the simple yet powerful markup language that is used in building Silverlight applications.

You'll notice that the properties of a button control can be set in XAML. The text that appears on the button is provided as the content of the button control. There are two important XAML syntaxes you should be aware of:

- **Attribute element syntax:** You can use this syntax to assign values to the properties of the control. In the previous XAML example, the width and height attributes have their values specified in the XAML itself.

- **Property element syntax:** The alternative way to assign values to the properties of a control is to use the property element syntax. Using the property element syntax, the XAML example above can be rewritten as

```
<Page
  xmlns="http://schemas.microsoft.com/winfx/2006/xaml/presentation"
  xmlns:x="http://schemas.microsoft.com/winfx/2006/xaml">
  <Grid>
    <Button x:Name="myButton" >
      <Button.Content>"Hello, World!"</Button.Content>
      <Button.Width>120</Button.Width>
      <Button.Height>40</Button.Height>
    </Button>
  </Grid>
</Page>
```

Note that you can assign a unique identifier to the button using the x:Name property. The unique identifier is useful in referencing the button in code.

Figure 7-2: A Silverlight page in Kaxaml.

XAML provides the ability to connect events that are defined in code with the user-interface elements. For example, if you want to change the text of the button when it's pressed, you define the following event handler in code:

```
private void Button_Click(object sender, RoutedEventArgs e)
{
    myButton.Content = "I am a button";
}
```

Figure 7-3 shows the button before it is clicked (with "Hello, World!" as the text set in the XAML) and after it is clicked (with the text set in the event handler).

Figure 7-3: A button updated by an event handler when clicked.

As is true with XML documents, a XAML document has only one top-level element. In the preceding example, this is the `<Page>` `</Page>` element. A number of namespaces are added to a XAML document that describe it as a Silverlight page. You'll find two namespaces in the preceding example, noted with the `xmlns` prefix. These namespaces are required in any Silverlight page to access essential components of the Silverlight runtime.

When you create a new application in Silverlight for Windows Phone 7 using Visual Studio, the elements of a page are embedded in a `<phone:Phone ApplicationPage>` `</phone:PhoneApplicationPage>` element. The XAML and design view of a page in a Windows Phone 7 application are show in Figure 7-4.

In this section, we introduce XAML and its features. You can find more about XAML and event handlers in Chapter 8, where you build your first application for Windows Phone 7.

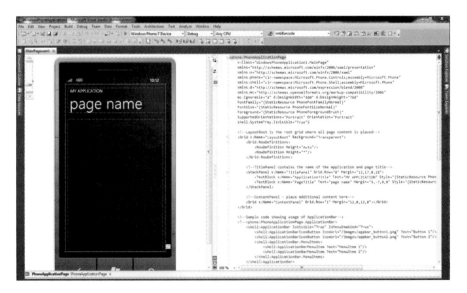

Figure 7-4: The XAML and design view of a page in a Windows Phone application.

Creating Animations

The preceding section shows you how XAML is used to create the look and feel of a Silverlight application. You can also use XAML to create animations. Animations make an application look more interactive and user-friendly. They can simplify various tasks, such as navigating through the application. Animations in Silverlight can be created purely in XAML and integrated with elements such as a button or an ellipse in a page.

An animation is considered to be an ordered set of frames that are viewed by the user in a sequence. Animations in Silverlight are created by changing the value of properties of user-interface elements such as the color of a rectangle, size of an ellipse, and so on over a period of time. Animations in Silverlight can be classified into two broad categories:

- ✔ **Property value animations:** These types of animations specify the initial value of a property, the final value after the animation is complete, and the value of each step in the animation. The value of the property varies continuously over the duration of the animation.

- ✔ **Keyframe animations:** In keyframe animations, the value of a property is set for specific intervals of time. Interpolation is used to calculate the value of the property between the keyframes.

Both types of animations are controlled by a storyboard. A storyboard can be used to group animations on an element. An animation is defined in XAML with a storyboard and an animation class such as `DoubleAnimation`. The `DoubleAnimation` class animates the value of a property by linear interpolation between two values over a specified duration.

Here's the XAML of a simple animation:

```
<Canvas xmlns="http://schemas.microsoft.com/client/2007"
xmlns:x="http://schemas.microsoft.com/winfx/2006/xaml">

    <Canvas.Triggers>
        <EventTrigger RoutedEvent="Canvas.Loaded" >
            <EventTrigger.Actions>
                <BeginStoryboard>
                    <Storyboard x:Name="animationHeight"
            Storyboard.TargetName="ellipse"
            Storyboard.TargetProperty="Height" RepeatBehavior="Forever" >
                        <DoubleAnimation To="80" Duration="0:0:10" />
                    </Storyboard>
                </BeginStoryboard>
                <BeginStoryboard>
                    <Storyboard x:Name="animationWidth"
            Storyboard.TargetName="ellipse"
            Storyboard.TargetProperty="Width" RepeatBehavior="Forever" >
                        <DoubleAnimation To="80" Duration="0:0:10" />
                    </Storyboard>
                </BeginStoryboard>
            </EventTrigger.Actions>
        </EventTrigger>
    </Canvas.Triggers>

    <Ellipse x:Name="ellipse" Height="20" Width="20" Canvas.Left="20"
            Canvas.Top="20" Fill="Red" />

</Canvas>
```

In this animation, the height and width of an ellipse is varied from 20 to 80 over 10 seconds. The animation is repeated continuously after it's triggered when the Canvas is loaded. The Canvas is the top-level element in the Silverlight page. The various steps in the animation are shown in Figure 7-5.

Figure 7-5: A simple animation in Silverlight.

In this simple example, we show how XAML can be used to create animations on user-interface elements such as an ellipse. XAML allows designers and developers to create animations in Silverlight applications. Animations can be created in Windows Phone 7 applications using XAML similar to the example described earlier.

You can watch a video about animations in Windows Phone 7 at http://bit.ly/eBTkjD.

Accessing Data in Silverlight

Earlier, we show you how XAML is used to declare user-interface elements and assign their properties. An important feature of XAML is *data binding*, a powerful way of connecting your user interface with a data source. Data binding allows the application to maintain a clean boundary between the user interface and its data source(s).

Data binding also enables properties of user-interface elements to be linked with XAML. A simple example of element-to-element data binding is illustrated with the following XAML:

```
<Grid xmlns="http://schemas.microsoft.com/client/2007"
      xmlns:x="http://schemas.microsoft.com/winfx/2006/xaml"
      Width="300"
      Height="300">

    <Grid.RowDefinitions>
        <RowDefinition Height="Auto" />
        <RowDefinition Height="Auto" />
        <RowDefinition Height="*" />
    </Grid.RowDefinitions>
    <Slider x:Name="slider" Grid.Row="0" Margin="8" Minimum="40" Maximum="80"
        Value="10" />
```

```
        <TextBlock x:Name="sliderValue" Grid.Row="1" Margin="8" FontSize="16"
                Text="{Binding ElementName=slider, Path=Value}" />
        <Ellipse x:Name="ellipse" Grid.Row="2" Height="{Binding
                ElementName=slider, Path=Value}" Width="{Binding
                ElementName=slider, Path=Value}" Fill="Red" />

    </Grid>
```

In the preceding XAML, a slider is used to control the width and height of an ellipse. Data binding uses the current value of the slider control and sets it to the width and height of the ellipse. In addition, the current value of the slider is displayed in the TextBlock. When the slider is moved, the current value is displayed in the TextBlock and the size of the ellipse changes (see Figure 7-6).

In this example, data binding sets the current value of the slider (the source) in the TextBlock and ellipse (the targets). This is one-way data binding. With XAML and data binding, you can have the data flow in both directions — that is, from source to target and vice versa. This is known as two-way data binding. The following XAML code illustrates a simple example of two-way data binding:

```
<Grid xmlns="http://schemas.microsoft.com/client/2007"
        xmlns:x="http://schemas.microsoft.com/winfx/2006/xaml"
        Width="300"
        Height="300">

    <Grid.RowDefinitions>
        <RowDefinition Height="Auto" />
        <RowDefinition Height="Auto" />
        <RowDefinition Height="Auto" />
    </Grid.RowDefinitions>
    <Slider x:Name="slider" Grid.Row="0" Margin="8" Minimum="40" Maximum="80"
            Value="10" />
    <TextBlock x:Name="sliderValue" Grid.Row="1" Margin="8" FontSize="16"
            Text="{Binding ElementName=slider, Path=Value}" />
    <TextBox x:Name="textbox" Grid.Row="2" Margin="8" FontSize="16"
            Height="30" Text="{Binding ElementName=slider, Path=Value,
            Mode=TwoWay}" />

    </Grid>
```

In this example, the TextBox is bound to the slider in a two-way binding mode. The value of the slider can be set by typing in the TextBox, and the value in the TextBox can be changed by the slider. Note that the TextBlock displays the current value of the slider. Two-way data binding is shown in Figure 7-7.

Data binding is very important in connecting properties of various user-interface elements using XAML without any code. Often, the designer can update the user interface without the need for the developer. This helps in the maintainability of the application.

Data binding is used in XAML to connect the data source with element(s) in the user interface of an application. The user-interface elements can be referred in code and data binding can be used in the code to connect them to their data source.

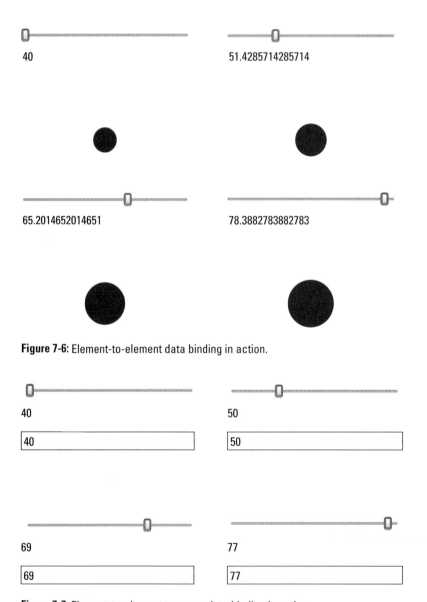

Figure 7-6: Element-to-element data binding in action.

Figure 7-7: Element-to-element two-way data binding in action.

Part III
Practicing with Simple Sample Apps

The 5th Wave   By Rich Tennant

Cell Phones

"This model comes with a particularly useful app — a simulated static button for breaking out of long-winded conversations."

In this part . . .

A tourist in New York City asks a policeman, "Excuse me, officer. Can you tell me how to get to Carnegie Hall?" The officer replies, "Practice, practice, practice!"

You can read all you want about writing applications, but there is no substitute for getting some practice with real apps, even if they do some very simple things.

Practice is what this part is about. We give you some experience writing real apps that use key aspects of Windows Phone 7. After you've successfully written these apps, you'll be better prepared for writing apps of your own.

Photo credits: Corbis Digital Stock (top, middle, bottom)

8

Breaking the Ice with Your First Application

In This Chapter

▶ Building a simple Windows Phone app

▶ Testing your app

▶ Getting your app ready for submission to the Marketplace

*I*n Chapter 5, we tell you how to download and install the Windows Phone Developer Tools. In this chapter, we take a closer look at these tools and build a simple application that you could submit to the Windows Phone Marketplace (although it's probably too simple to get many downloads if you were to take it that far!).

The app we walk you through in this chapter starts with its background color set to gold and the button's background color set to light gray. When the button is pressed, the background colors of both the app and the button change. The background colors toggle between the two every time the button is pressed. The color is toggled when the event handler for the Click event of the button is fired. The background colors are changed by swapping them in the event handler.

The Windows Phone Developer Tools have a simple and easy-to-use interface. You can build an app with a simple interface in a matter of hours and get it ready for the Marketplace. Here's an overview of the steps you take when building a Windows Phone app:

PhotoDisc/Getty Images

1. **Open Visual Studio, and create a new Windows Phone project.**

   In most cases, you select the Windows Phone Application template from the list of templates and create a new project.

2. **Use the designer in Visual Studio to add the controls in your app and build the user interface.**

3. **Write the code that will run when event handlers from these controls are fired.**

4. **Build, run, and test your application.**

   You build and run your app on the Windows Phone Emulator and, wherever necessary, a real device. You also test the app's XAP file on a real device before uploading to the Marketplace.

5. **Prepare for Marketplace submission.**

   After you've successfully tested the app, create artwork that goes with the app, and upload it with the app's XAP file to the Marketplace.

In this chapter, we walk you through these steps with a sample app. This exercise prepares you to create the app you've always dreamed of.

Writing the Code

In this section, we walk you through the steps to create the application's user interface using Visual Studio and write the code that will change the background color of the application and the button.

Creating an app and updating its user interface

Follow these steps to create a new project in Visual Studio and update its user interface:

1. **Open Visual Studio, and select File⇨New⇨Project.**

   The New Project dialog box appears.

2. **Click Silverlight for Windows Phone in the left column and then select the Windows Phone Application template, as shown in Figure 8-1.**

3. **Name your project ColorToggle (or any other name you like) and click OK.**

   After the project is created, `MainPage.xaml` opens. Other files from the project are listed in the Solution Explorer window, as shown in Figure 8-2.

   You can click the Solution Explorer and drag and dock to any region within Visual Studio. You also can double-click the Solution Explorer to detach it from the main window.

Figure 8-1: Select the Windows Phone Application template.

Figure 8-2: The Visual Studio application with the ColorToggle project open.

4. Hover your mouse over the Toolbox menu on the left side of Visual Studio.

The Toolbox pane opens, as shown in Figure 8-3.

Figure 8-3: Visual Studio with the Toolbox pane open.

5. Drag and drop a Button control from the Toolbox pane into the application.

You see the button anchored to the left and top of the main window, as shown in Figure 8-4. Now you can update a few properties of the Button control.

6. Right-click the button and select Properties, as shown in Figure 8-5.

The Properties window opens.

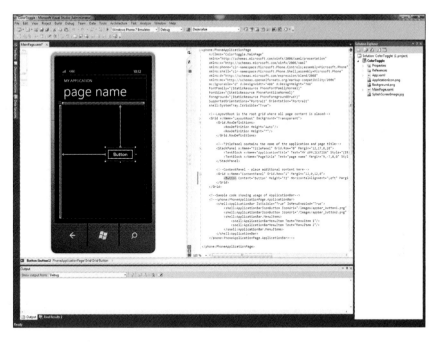

Figure 8-4: The Button control in the application.

Figure 8-5: Open the Button control's properties.

7. **Locate the Content property and change the value to Toggle.**

8. **Select a color for the background of the button using the Color Picker, as shown in Figure 8-6.**

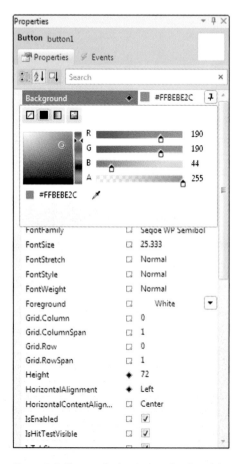

Figure 8-6: Change the background color of the button.

Be sure to pick the Solid Color Brush from the top left of the Color Picker dialog box (it's the second item from the left).

You can move the button to the center of the application by holding it down and pushing it toward the center.

9. **To delete the Page Name TextBlock, right-click it and select Delete, as shown in Figure 8-7.**

Figure 8-7: Delete the Page Name TextBlock.

10. **Right-click the My Application title TextBlock and change its Text property to Color Toggle, as shown in Figure 8-8.**

11. **Click the edge of the application's area to select the outermost Grid, and right-click the Grid to select the Properties window.**

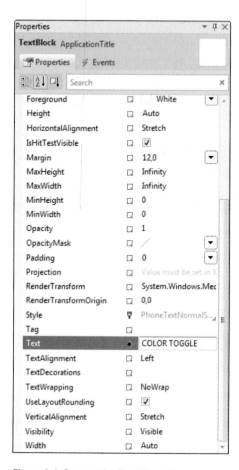

Figure 8-8: Change the TextBlock Text property to COLOR TOGGLE.

After you've selected the outermost Grid, you see it highlighted, as shown in Figure 8-9.

12. Select a light gray color for the background of the application using the Color Picker.

13. Update the XAML for the button.

The button you've added in XAML will swap its background color with the background color of the application. In order for this to work, you need to update the XAML of the button in `MainPage.xaml.cs` with the following:

Figure 8-9: The outermost Grid of the application selected.

```
<Button Content="Toggle" Height="72" HorizontalAlignment="Left"
        Margin="143,220,0,0"
            Name="button1" VerticalAlignment="Top"
Width="160" Background="#FFBEBE2C" Click="button1_Click">
        <Button.Template>
            <ControlTemplate TargetType="Button">
                <Grid Background="Transparent">
                    <VisualStateManager.VisualStateGroups>
                        <VisualStateGroup x:Name="CommonStates">
                            <VisualState x:Name="Normal"/>
                            <VisualState x:Name="MouseOver"/>
                            <VisualState x:Name="Pressed">
                                <Storyboard>
                                    <ObjectAnimationUsingKeyFrames
        Storyboard.TargetName="ContentContainer"
        Storyboard.TargetProperty="Foreground">
                                        <DiscreteObjectKeyFrame KeyTime="0"
        Value="{StaticResource PhoneBackgroundBrush}" />
                                    </ObjectAnimationUsingKeyFrames>
                                    <ObjectAnimationUsingKeyFrames
        Storyboard.TargetName="PressedHighlightBackground"
        Storyboard.TargetProperty="Background">
```

(continued)

(continued)

```xml
<DiscreteObjectKeyFrame KeyTime="0" Value="{StaticResource
    PhoneForegroundBrush}" />
                        </ObjectAnimationUsingKeyFrames>
                        <ObjectAnimationUsingKeyFrames
    Storyboard.TargetName="ButtonBackground"
    Storyboard.TargetProperty="BorderBrush">
                            <DiscreteObjectKeyFrame KeyTime="0"
    Value="{StaticResource PhoneForegroundBrush}" />
                        </ObjectAnimationUsingKeyFrames>
                    </Storyboard>
                </VisualState>
                <VisualState x:Name="Disabled">
                    <Storyboard>
                        <ObjectAnimationUsingKeyFrames
    Storyboard.TargetName="ContentContainer"
    Storyboard.TargetProperty="Foreground">
                            <DiscreteObjectKeyFrame KeyTime="0"
    Value="{StaticResource PhoneDisabledBrush}" />
                        </ObjectAnimationUsingKeyFrames>
                        <ObjectAnimationUsingKeyFrames
    Storyboard.TargetName="ButtonBackground"
    Storyboard.TargetProperty="BorderBrush">
                            <DiscreteObjectKeyFrame KeyTime="0"
    Value="{StaticResource PhoneDisabledBrush}" />
                        </ObjectAnimationUsingKeyFrames>
                        <ObjectAnimationUsingKeyFrames
    Storyboard.TargetName="ButtonBackground"
    Storyboard.TargetProperty="Background">
                            <DiscreteObjectKeyFrame KeyTime="0"
    Value="Transparent" />
                        </ObjectAnimationUsingKeyFrames>
                    </Storyboard>
                </VisualState>
            </VisualStateGroup>
        </VisualStateManager.VisualStateGroups>
        <Border x:Name="ButtonBackground"
BorderBrush="{TemplateBinding BorderBrush}"            Bor
derThickness="{TemplateBinding BorderThickness}"
CornerRadius="0"            Background="{TemplateBinding
Background}" Margin="{StaticResource PhoneTouchTargetOverhang}"
>
            <Border x:Name="PressedHighlightBackground"
Background="Transparent">
                <ContentControl x:Name="ContentContainer"
Foreground="{TemplateBinding Foreground}" HorizontalAlign
ment="{TemplateBinding HorizontalContentAlignment}" Verti
calAlignment="{TemplateBinding VerticalContentAlignment}"
Padding="{TemplateBinding Padding}"
Content="{TemplateBinding Content}" ContentTemplate="{TemplateBi
nding ContentTemplate}"/>
            </Border>
        </Border>
    </Grid>
```

```
                            </ControlTemplate>
                        </Button.Template>
                    </Button>
```

We had to modify the default template of the button in the last step — the background color change when the button is clicked is not visible to the user because the change is hidden by animations. If you're interested in the details, head over to Peter Torr's blog post at `http://bit.ly/jJBj4P`.

You've finished updating the application's user interface.

Creating an event handler

To create an event handler that will be fired for the `Click` event of the button, follow these steps:

1. **Open the Properties window of the button and click the Events tab, shown in Figure 8-10.**

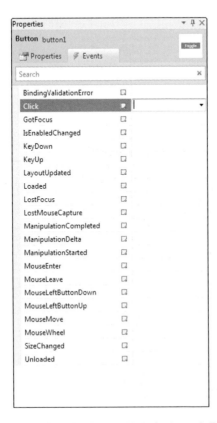

Figure 8-10: The Events tab in the button's Properties window.

2. Double-click the empty TextBox next to the `Click` event.

An event handler is created in the code file `MainPage.xaml.cs`, as follows:

```
private void button1_Click(object sender, RoutedEventArgs e)
{

}
```

This event handler is fired every time the button is clicked.

In the next few chapters, you work with XAML, and you need to understand the layout of the user interface from the XAML perspective. Here is the XAML of the application's user interface in `MainPage.xaml`:

```
<phone:PhoneApplicationPage
    x:Class="ColorToggle.MainPage"
    xmlns="http://schemas.microsoft.com/winfx/2006/xaml/presentation"
    xmlns:x="http://schemas.microsoft.com/winfx/2006/xaml"
    xmlns:phone="clr-namespace:Microsoft.Phone.Controls;assembly=Microsoft.
           Phone"
    xmlns:shell="clr-namespace:Microsoft.Phone.Shell;assembly=Microsoft.Phone"
    xmlns:d="http://schemas.microsoft.com/expression/blend/2008"
    xmlns:mc="http://schemas.openxmlformats.org/markup-compatibility/2006"
    mc:Ignorable="d" d:DesignWidth="480" d:DesignHeight="768"
    FontFamily="{StaticResource PhoneFontFamilyNormal}"
    FontSize="{StaticResource PhoneFontSizeNormal}"
    Foreground="{StaticResource PhoneForegroundBrush}"
    SupportedOrientations="Portrait" Orientation="Portrait"
    shell:SystemTray.IsVisible="True">
    <!--LayoutRoot is the root Grid where all page content is placed-->
    <Grid x:Name="LayoutRoot" Background="#FFA09494">
        <Grid.RowDefinitions>
            <RowDefinition Height="Auto"/>
            <RowDefinition Height="*"/>
        </Grid.RowDefinitions>

        <!--TitlePanel contains the name of the application and page title-->
        <StackPanel x:Name="TitlePanel" Grid.Row="0" Margin="12,17,0,28">
            <TextBlock x:Name="ApplicationTitle" Text="COLOR TOGGLE"
                Style="{StaticResource PhoneTextNormalStyle}"/>
        </StackPanel>

        <!--ContentPanel - place additional content here-->
        <Grid x:Name="ContentPanel" Grid.Row="1" Margin="12,0,12,0">

<Button Content="Toggle" Height="72" HorizontalAlignment="Left"
            Margin="143,220,0,0"
                Name="button1" VerticalAlignment="Top"
Width="160" Background="#FFBEBE2C" Click="button1_Click">
            <Button.Template>
                <ControlTemplate TargetType="Button">
```

```xml
<Grid Background="Transparent">
    <VisualStateManager.VisualStateGroups>
        <VisualStateGroup x:Name="CommonStates">
            <VisualState x:Name="Normal"/>
            <VisualState x:Name="MouseOver"/>
            <VisualState x:Name="Pressed">
                <Storyboard>
                    <ObjectAnimationUsingKeyFrames
Storyboard.TargetName="ContentContainer"
Storyboard.TargetProperty="Foreground">
                        <DiscreteObjectKeyFrame KeyTime="0"
Value="{StaticResource PhoneBackgroundBrush}" />
                    </ObjectAnimationUsingKeyFrames>
                    <ObjectAnimationUsingKeyFrames
Storyboard.TargetName="PressedHighlightBackground"
Storyboard.TargetProperty="Background">
                        <DiscreteObjectKeyFrame KeyTime="0"
Value="{StaticResource PhoneForegroundBrush}" />
                    </ObjectAnimationUsingKeyFrames>
                    <ObjectAnimationUsingKeyFrames
Storyboard.TargetName="ButtonBackground"
Storyboard.TargetProperty="BorderBrush">
                        <DiscreteObjectKeyFrame KeyTime="0"
Value="{StaticResource PhoneForegroundBrush}" />
                    </ObjectAnimationUsingKeyFrames>
                </Storyboard>
            </VisualState>
            <VisualState x:Name="Disabled">
                <Storyboard>
                    <ObjectAnimationUsingKeyFrames
Storyboard.TargetName="ContentContainer"
Storyboard.TargetProperty="Foreground">
                        <DiscreteObjectKeyFrame KeyTime="0"
Value="{StaticResource PhoneDisabledBrush}" />
                    </ObjectAnimationUsingKeyFrames>
                    <ObjectAnimationUsingKeyFrames
Storyboard.TargetName="ButtonBackground"
Storyboard.TargetProperty="BorderBrush">
                        <DiscreteObjectKeyFrame KeyTime="0"
Value="{StaticResource PhoneDisabledBrush}" />
                    </ObjectAnimationUsingKeyFrames>
                    <ObjectAnimationUsingKeyFrames
Storyboard.TargetName="ButtonBackground"
Storyboard.TargetProperty="Background">
                        <DiscreteObjectKeyFrame KeyTime="0"
Value="Transparent" />
                    </ObjectAnimationUsingKeyFrames>
                </Storyboard>
            </VisualState>
        </VisualStateGroup>
    </VisualStateManager.VisualStateGroups>
```

(continued)

(continued)

```
                <Border x:Name="ButtonBackground"
BorderBrush="{TemplateBinding BorderBrush}"                  Border
Thickness="{TemplateBinding BorderThickness}" CornerRadius="0"
Background="{TemplateBinding Background}" Margin="{StaticResource
PhoneTouchTargetOverhang}" >
                    <Border x:Name="PressedHighlightBackground"
Background="Transparent">
                        <ContentControl x:Name="ContentContainer"
Foreground="{TemplateBinding Foreground}" HorizontalAlignment="{Te
mplateBinding HorizontalContentAlignment}" VerticalAlignment="{Te
mplateBinding VerticalContentAlignment}" Padding="{TemplateBinding
Padding}"                      Content="{TemplateBinding Content}"
ContentTemplate="{TemplateBinding ContentTemplate}"/>
                    </Border>
                </Border>
            </Grid>
        </ControlTemplate>
      </Button.Template>
    </Button>          </Grid>
  </Grid>

<!--Sample code showing usage of ApplicationBar-->
<!--<phone:PhoneApplicationPage.ApplicationBar>
    <shell:ApplicationBar IsVisible="True" IsMenuEnabled="True">
        <shell:ApplicationBarIconButton IconUri="/Images/appbar_button1.png"
          Text="Button 1"/>
        <shell:ApplicationBarIconButton IconUri="/Images/appbar_button2.png"
          Text="Button 2"/>
        <shell:ApplicationBar.MenuItems>
            <shell:ApplicationBarMenuItem Text="MenuItem 1"/>
            <shell:ApplicationBarMenuItem Text="MenuItem 2"/>
        </shell:ApplicationBar.MenuItems>
    </shell:ApplicationBar>
</phone:PhoneApplicationPage.ApplicationBar>-->

</phone:PhoneApplicationPage>
```

There are two important points to note in the XAML:

- **The main layout Grid:** A Grid is fundamental in arranging the layout of the application. Every new page you create for an application will have a Grid as the main element. Other user interface elements are embedded in this Grid.

- **Event handlers for controls:** Event handlers for controls are usually wired through XAML, which helps in understanding the interaction of various controls in the user interface.

In the next section, you add code to the event handler of the button's `Click` event.

Using the editor

Open the `MainPage.xaml.cs` file, and update the event handler with the following code:

```
private void button1_Click(object sender, RoutedEventArgs e)
{
    Brush layoutBackground = LayoutRoot.Background;
    LayoutRoot.Background = button1.Background;
    button1.Background = layoutBackground;
}
```

In the event handler, the current value of the main layout Grid's background is saved in a variable. The Grid's background is then set to the button's background. In the last step, the button's background is set to the value stored in the temporary variable. Your application is ready to be tested in the Windows Phone Emulator.

Testing Your App in the Windows Phone Emulator

The Windows Phone Emulator ships as part of the Windows Phone Developer Tools. You can start it using the shortcut within Windows Phone Developer Tools — just click Windows Phone Emulator.

Alternatively, you can start the emulator by selecting the Windows Phone 7 Emulator as the target in Visual Studio and clicking the Debug button (see Figure 8-11).

Figure 8-11: Opening the Windows Phone Emulator in Visual Studio.

After the emulator starts, your application is deployed in it and started. Figure 8-12 shows the ColorToggle application running in the emulator.

Click the toggle button to check if the color of the button's background and the color of the application's background are swapped. Figure 8-13 shows the application running in the emulator with the colors toggled.

Now that you've verified that the application's features are working as expected, it's time to start bundling the application for submission.

Figure 8-12: The ColorToggle application running in the emulator.

Figure 8-13: The ColorToggle application with the background colors toggled.

Bundling Your App for Submission

Chapter 16 goes through the submission process, but before you get to that point, you need to prepare your app for submission. The Windows Phone Marketplace guidelines require you to update the capabilities of the app so that only the necessary capabilities are present in the application's manifest file. The manifest file, called `WMAppManifest.xml`, is present in the Properties group in the Solution Explorer. Here's the original manifest file for the ColorToggle app:

```xml
<?xml version="1.0" encoding="utf-8"?>

<Deployment xmlns="http://schemas.microsoft.com/windowsphone/2009/deployment"
            AppPlatformVersion="7.0">
  <App xmlns="" ProductID="{2216d469-34d4-40eb-881c-672f17a0052e}"
            Title="ColorToggle" RuntimeType="Silverlight" Version="1.0.0.0"
            Genre="apps.normal" Author="ColorToggle author"
            Description="Sample description" Publisher="ColorToggle">
    <IconPath IsRelative="true" IsResource="false">ApplicationIcon.png</
            IconPath>
```

```
  <Capabilities>
    <Capability Name="ID_CAP_GAMERSERVICES"/>
    <Capability Name="ID_CAP_IDENTITY_DEVICE"/>
    <Capability Name="ID_CAP_IDENTITY_USER"/>
    <Capability Name="ID_CAP_LOCATION"/>
    <Capability Name="ID_CAP_MEDIALIB"/>
    <Capability Name="ID_CAP_MICROPHONE"/>
    <Capability Name="ID_CAP_NETWORKING"/>
    <Capability Name="ID_CAP_PHONEDIALER"/>
    <Capability Name="ID_CAP_PUSH_NOTIFICATION"/>
    <Capability Name="ID_CAP_SENSORS"/>
    <Capability Name="ID_CAP_WEBBROWSERCOMPONENT"/>
  </Capabilities>
  <Tasks>
    <DefaultTask  Name ="_default" NavigationPage="MainPage.xaml"/>
  </Tasks>
  <Tokens>
    <PrimaryToken TokenID="ColorToggleToken" TaskName="_default">
      <TemplateType5>
        <BackgroundImageURI IsRelative="true" IsResource="false">Background.
          png</BackgroundImageURI>
        <Count>0</Count>
        <Title>ColorToggle</Title>
      </TemplateType5>
    </PrimaryToken>
  </Tokens>
  </App>
</Deployment>
```

Note that the manifest file includes all the capabilities available for an application. In the ColorToggle app, we aren't using any of the capabilities listed. So, you need to remove all the capabilities, recompile the application, and test it before starting the submission process.

In the final step of testing, you'll prepare the XAP file of the app and deploy it in the emulator or a real Windows Phone device. In order to test your app with a real Windows Phone, make sure the phone is connected and the screen lock is turned off. Then follow these steps:

1. **In Visual Studio, switch the build mode to Release and recompile the application.**

2. **From within the Windows Phone Developer Tools program option on your PC, select the Application Deployment shortcut.**

   The Application Deployment window appears (see Figure 8-14).

3. **In the Target drop-down list, select Windows Phone Emulator.**

Figure 8-14: The Application Deployment window.

4. **Click the Browse button to open the XAP file.**

   Your application's XAP file can be found in the `Bin\Release` folder of the project.

5. **Click Deploy.**

   The tool will deploy the XAP file to the emulator and start it.

Test your app a few times to ensure that it's working properly.

Because the default icons and the background file that ship with the Visual Studio Windows Phone template are not very attractive, you may want to update them in your project. Remember to close Visual Studio and overwrite the PNG icon files and the JPG splash screen.

If you encounter any issues (for example, the icons or the splash screen are not visible), check the properties of these files in Visual Studio. Their Build Action property must be set to Content, and the Copy to Output Directory must be set to Copy Always or Copy If Newer.

After you've ensured that the app is working as you expect, prepare some screenshots of the app and the app tile artwork, and get ready to upload your app through the App Hub (see Chapter 16).

9

Creating a Simple Calculation App

In This Chapter

▶ Designing the user interface with the Metro theme in mind

▶ Using swipe gestures in your application

▶ Detecting shake motion with the accelerometer

*W*indows Phone 7 ships with a calculator useful for simple calculations. People often encounter situations in which they need to work with a single number — halving it, doubling it, or squaring it. So, in this chapter, you build an application that lets the user enter a number and then doubles the number when the user swipes right, halves the number when the user swipes left, and squares the number when the user shakes the phone. We call the app SwipeNShakeCalc.

The goal here is to break the ice with a simple app that you can use to learn how to work with the tools you've downloaded. This chapter helps lay the groundwork for you to make more complex apps.

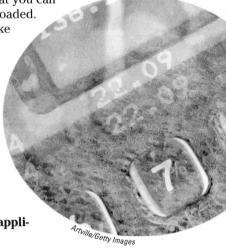
Artville/Getty Images

Creating the User Interface

In the SwipeNShakeCalc app, you need the following elements in the user interface:

▶ **A TextBox to enter the number:** When the user wants to enter the input value, the on-screen keyboard will allow only digits to be entered.

▶ **A TextBlock to hint to the user how to use the application:** The app will show the following text:

swipe right to double

swipe left to halve

shake to square

This text will help the user perform calculations.

✔ **A TextBlock that shows the last operation performed:** This TextBlock will display the operation performed by the user. It will display text like 24/2 =.

✔ **A TextBlock to display the result:** The app will display the result in this TextBlock. We use a large font style to make the result prominent in the application's interface.

In order to lay out the four user interface elements in the application, we use a Grid with four rows, one row for each element. The layout will use the height of the elements to occupy the height of each row in the Grid, except for the TextBlock that shows a hint on how to use the application. This TextBlock will occupy the rest of the vertical space in the Grid after it has been distributed across the three elements.

An important point in the Metro design principle is a clean layout with legible fonts. In the SwipeNShakeCalc app, we use system styles to set the font size and font colors. The font sizes used in the app won't leave much white space between the user interface elements. You probably need to work with the font sizes before you settle on the right set of font sizes for the elements. Figure 9-1 shows the app as seen in the Visual Studio designer. Note how the TextBlock that provides a hint to the user on how to use the application occupies the rest of the space in the Grid.

Figure 9-1: The SwipeNShakeCalc user interface.

TIP

We use system styles in all the elements except the TextBox. You can refer to the article at `http://bit.ly/dByZDj` to find out more about system styles and how to use them in your app.

Creating the Application

Follow these steps to create your new project in Visual Studio:

1. **Open Visual Studio, and select File⇨New⇨Project.**

   The New Project dialog box appears.

2. **Click Silverlight for Windows Phone in the left column and then select the Windows Phone Application template.**

3. **Name your project SwipeNShakeCalc (see Figure 9-2), and click OK.**

Figure 9-2: Create a new project for SwipeNShakeCalc.

In the following sections, we walk you through how to add assemblies, put together the app's main page, validate the user's input, and do the math.

Adding assemblies

Because we'll be using the accelerometer for shake detection, you need to add a reference to the `Microsoft.Devices.Sensors` assembly:

1. **Right-click the project, and select Add Reference.**

   The Add Reference dialog box opens.

2. **Select the `Microsoft.Devices.Sensors` assembly (see Figure 9-3), and click OK.**

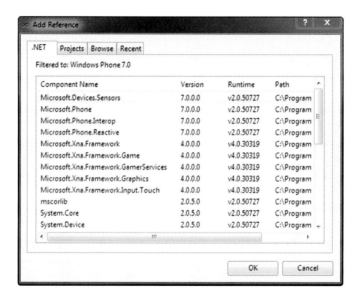

Figure 9-3: Add the `Microsoft.Devices.Sensors` assembly to the project.

You'll be using swipe gestures in the application to perform some operations. The Windows Phone 7 API doesn't provide any support for touch gestures (swiping, double tapping, single tapping, and so on). Therefore, you need to use the Silverlight for Windows Phone Controls Toolkit, available at http:// silverlight.codeplex.com. After you've installed the toolkit, add a reference to the `Microsoft.Phone.Controls.Toolkit` assembly by following the same steps as you did to add the reference to the `Microsoft.Devices. Sensors` assembly. Note that you'll need to scroll to the bottom of the dialog box in order to add the assembly (see Figure 9-4).

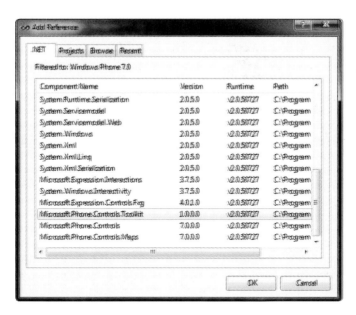

Figure 9-4: Add the `Microsoft.Phone.Controls.Toolkit`
assembly to the project.

Putting together the app's main page

Now that you've added all the necessary assemblies into your project, you
can create the main page of the application. The XAML of the main page
looks like this:

```
<phone:PhoneApplicationPage
    x:Class="SwipeNShakeCalc.MainPage"
    xmlns="http://schemas.microsoft.com/winfx/2006/xaml/presentation"
    xmlns:x="http://schemas.microsoft.com/winfx/2006/xaml"
    xmlns:phone="clr-namespace:Microsoft.Phone.Controls;assembly=Microsoft.
            Phone"
    xmlns:shell="clr-namespace:Microsoft.Phone.Shell;assembly=Microsoft.Phone"
    xmlns:d="http://schemas.microsoft.com/expression/blend/2008"
    xmlns:mc="http://schemas.openxmlformats.org/markup-compatibility/2006"
    xmlns:toolkit="clr-namespace:Microsoft.Phone.Controls;assembly=Microsoft.
            Phone.Controls.Toolkit"
    mc:Ignorable="d" d:DesignWidth="480" d:DesignHeight="768"
    FontFamily="{StaticResource PhoneFontFamilyNormal}"
    FontSize="{StaticResource PhoneFontSizeNormal}"
    Foreground="{StaticResource PhoneForegroundBrush}"
    SupportedOrientations="Portrait" Orientation="Portrait"
    shell:SystemTray.IsVisible="True">
```

(continued)

(continued)

```xml
<!--LayoutRoot is the root Grid where all page content is placed-->
<Grid x:Name="LayoutRoot" Background="Transparent">
    <Grid.RowDefinitions>
        <RowDefinition Height="Auto"/>
        <RowDefinition Height="*"/>
    </Grid.RowDefinitions>

    <!--TitlePanel contains the name of the application and page title-->
    <StackPanel x:Name="TitlePanel" Grid.Row="0" Margin="12,17,0,28">
        <TextBlock x:Name="ApplicationTitle" Text="SWIPENSHAKECALC"
            Style="{StaticResource PhoneTextNormalStyle}"/>
    </StackPanel>

    <!--ContentPanel - place additional content here-->
    <Grid x:Name="ContentPanel" Grid.Row="1" Margin="12,0,12,0">
        <Grid.RowDefinitions>
            <RowDefinition Height="Auto" />
            <RowDefinition Height="*" />
            <RowDefinition Height="Auto" />
            <RowDefinition Height="Auto" />
        </Grid.RowDefinitions>
        <TextBox x:Name="InputValue" Margin="9,0,0,0" Padding="14,0,0,0"
                Text="2.0"
                FontSize="72"
                Grid.Row="0">
            <TextBox.InputScope>
                <InputScope>
                    <InputScopeName NameValue="TelephoneNumber" />
                </InputScope>
            </TextBox.InputScope>
        </TextBox>
        <TextBlock Margin="9,0,0,0" Padding="2,0,0,0"
                Text="swipe right to double swipe left to halve shake to
            square"
                TextWrapping="Wrap"
                VerticalAlignment="Center"
                TextAlignment="Center"
                Style="{StaticResource PhoneTextExtraLargeStyle}"
                Grid.Row="1" />
        <TextBlock x:Name="Operation" Margin="9,0,0,0" Padding="30,0,0,0"
                Text="2.0/2 ="
                Style="{StaticResource PhoneTextExtraLargeStyle}"
                Foreground="{StaticResource PhoneAccentBrush}"
                Grid.Row="2" />
        <TextBlock x:Name="Result" Margin="9,-20,0,0" Padding="20,0,0,0"
                Text="1.0"
                Style="{StaticResource PhoneTextHugeStyle}"
                Foreground="{StaticResource PhoneAccentBrush}"
                Grid.Row="3"/>
        <toolkit:GestureService.GestureListener>
            <toolkit:GestureListener Flick="OnSwipe" />
        </toolkit:GestureService.GestureListener>
```

```
        </Grid>
    </Grid>

</phone:PhoneApplicationPage>
```

In the XAML, we've removed the section for the application bar because you won't be using it in the SwipeNShakeCalc application. Note that we've added an import statement for the Windows Phone Controls Toolkit:

```
xmlns:toolkit="clr-namespace:Microsoft.Phone.Controls;assembly=Microsoft.Phone.
                Controls.Toolkit"
```

This allows us to connect the event handler for the swipe gestures we'll use for the calculation operation:

```
<toolkit:GestureService.GestureListener>
        <toolkit:GestureListener Flick="OnSwipe" />
        </toolkit:GestureService.GestureListener>
```

Left and right swipe actions are handled in the `OnSwipe` event handler.

You may have noticed that the TextBox used to input numbers in the application has an `InputScope` associated with it. The `InputScopeName` enumeration modifies how the software input keyboard is laid out when the user clicks the TextBox. A full list of the various layouts available for the keyboard is available at `http://bit.ly/bOQ8Aw`. The software input keyboard as it appears when the app is running is shown in Figure 9-5.

You also may have noticed that we're using the `TelephoneNumber` enumeration for the keyboard layout. This layout prevents the user from entering letters and other characters through the keyboard, which simplifies the input validation of the entered number (see the next section for more on input validation).

Now that the user interface is ready and all the necessary assemblies are available in the project, we'll add the code that will provide the functionality to the app. First, we'll build the logic to handle the swipe actions; then we'll add the logic for the shake motion.

Validating the user's input

When the user taps the TextBox to enter a number, the numeric keyboard appears. We selected the `TelephoneNumber` enumeration for the keyboard layout because it provides fewer characters to input than other layouts. This keyboard layout has a few non-numerical characters that we need to check for before performing any operation on the number entered. The invalid characters are

```
   *      +       ,       #

   (     )       ×       −
```

The + appears when you hold down the 0 key. The four characters on the second row (the two parentheses, ×, and −) appear when the decimal key is held down.

Figure 9-5: SwipeNShakeCalc with the software input keyboard visible.

The user may enter multiple decimal characters in the TextBox using the keyboard, so this needs to be checked.

We'll write a method that will be used by various event handlers to validate the number entered by the user. This method, `ValidateInput`, will return true if the number entered in the TextBox is a valid number; otherwise, it will return false. It will be added to the `MainPage` class in the `MainPage.xaml.cs` file.

```
/// <summary>
/// This method validates the number input by user for calculation
/// </summary>
/// <param name="inputNumber"></param>
/// <returns></returns>
```

```
private bool ValidateInput(string inputNumber)
{
    string[] invalidCharacters = { "*", "#", ",", "(", ")", "x", "-", "+",
        " " };

    // Check for invalid characters
    for (int i = 0; i < invalidCharacters.Length; i++)
    {
        if (inputNumber.Contains(invalidCharacters[i]))
        {
            return false;
        }
    }

    // Multiple decimals
    int decimalCount = inputNumber.Length - inputNumber.Replace(".", "").
        Length;
    if (decimalCount > 1) // More than one decimal character is present
        return false;

    return true;
}
```

Now that we have a way to validate the user's input, we'll set up the event handlers to perform calculations on the number.

Doubling when you swipe to the right, halving when you swipe to the left

Swipe gestures on the Windows Phone raise the `Flick` event on the `GestureListener` we've set up in the main layout Grid. In the event handler, the `FlickGestureEventArgs` event arguments provide the horizontal velocity, vertical velocity, angle, and direction of the flick gesture. In the event handler, we'll check the value of the horizontal velocity to determine if the flick gesture was toward the left or toward the right. This allows us to eliminate spurious gesture events from being generated.

Here's the code that handles a swipe to the right:

```
// Swipe right : Multiply by 2
if (e.HorizontalVelocity > 0)
{
    if (ValidateInput(InputValue.Text))
    {
        double enteredNumber;
        if (double.TryParse(InputValue.Text, out enteredNumber))
        {
            double result = enteredNumber * 2.0;
            Operation.Text = InputValue.Text + " * 2 = ";
            Result.Text = result.ToString();
```

(continued)

(continued)

```
            }
        }
        else
        {
            Operation.Text = "Please enter a valid number";
        }
    }
```

The code validates the number entered by the user, calculates the result, and updates the two TextBlocks.

Here's the code that handles a swipe gesture to the left:

```
// Swipe left : Divide by 2
    if (e.HorizontalVelocity < 0)
    {
        if (ValidateInput(InputValue.Text))
        {
            double enteredNumber;
            if (double.TryParse(InputValue.Text, out enteredNumber))
            {
                double result = enteredNumber / 2.0;
                Operation.Text = InputValue.Text + " / 2 = ";
                Result.Text = result.ToString();
            }
        }
        else
        {
            Operation.Text = "Please enter a valid number";
        }
    }
```

Here's the complete event handler for the swipe gestures, which should be located in the `MainPage` class:

```
private void OnSwipe(object sender, FlickGestureEventArgs e)
    {
        // Dismiss the keyboard, if visible
        this.Focus();

        // Swipe left : Divide by 2
        if (e.HorizontalVelocity < 0)
        {
            if (ValidateInput(InputValue.Text))
            {
                double enteredNumber;
                if (double.TryParse(InputValue.Text, out enteredNumber))
                {
                    double result = enteredNumber / 2.0;
                    Operation.Text = InputValue.Text + " / 2 = ";
                    Result.Text = result.ToString();
                }
```

```
        }
        else
        {
            Operation.Text = "Please enter a valid number";
        }
    }

    // Swipe right : Multiply by 2
    if (e.HorizontalVelocity > 0)
    {
        if (ValidateInput(InputValue.Text))
        {
            double enteredNumber;
            if (double.TryParse(InputValue.Text, out enteredNumber))
            {
                double result = enteredNumber * 2.0;
                Operation.Text = InputValue.Text + " * 2 = ";
                Result.Text = result.ToString();
            }
        }
        else
        {
            Operation.Text = "Please enter a valid number";
        }
    }
}
```

Squaring when you shake

To square the entered number, we'll use the shake motion of the phone.
In order to use the accelerometer, add the following code to the top of the
`MainPage.xaml.cs` file:

```
// Namespace imports for application
using Microsoft.Devices.Sensors;
```

Next, within the `MainPage` class in the `MainPage.xaml.cs` file, add the following code to declare some variables we'll soon use:

```
private const double _shakeThreshold = 0.5;
private Accelerometer _accelerometer;
private AccelerometerReadingEventArgs _lastAccelerometerReading;
private bool _shaking;
private int _shakeCount;
```

The accelerometer present in every Windows Phone device provides a
way to detect shake motion of the phone. We'll set up the accelerometer
in the constructor of the `MainPage` class with an event handler for the
`ReadingChanged` event. Here's the code that you need to add to the constructor of the `MainPage` class:

```
                // Set up the accelerometer for shake detection
        _accelerometer = new Accelerometer();
        _accelerometer.ReadingChanged += new EventHandler<AccelerometerReadingE
            ventArgs>(Accelerometer_ReadingChanged);
        _accelerometer.Start();
```

The `ReadingChanged` event is raised whenever a new reading from the accelerometer is obtained. The current reading obtained from the accelerometer is compared with the previous reading to detect if the phone has been shaken by the user.

Here's the code for the `ReadingChanged` event handler:

```
        /// <summary>
        /// This event handler is invoked whenever the readings from the
                accelerometer change.
        /// </summary>
        /// <param name="sender"></param>
        /// <param name="e"></param>
        void Accelerometer_ReadingChanged(object sender,
                AccelerometerReadingEventArgs e)
        {
            // Dismiss the keyboard, if visible.
            this.Dispatcher.BeginInvoke(() =>
            {
                this.Focus();
            });


            if (_accelerometer.State == SensorState.Ready)
            {
                AccelerometerReadingEventArgs currentAccelerometerReading = e;
                try
                {
                    if (_lastAccelerometerReading != null) // We can now check if the
                    phone was shaken by the user.
                    {
                        if (!_shaking && DetectShakeMotion(_lastAccelerometerReading,
                        currentAccelerometerReading, _shakeThreshold) && _shakeCount >= 1)
                        {
                            // Shake motion detected
                            _shaking = true;
                            _shakeCount = 0; // Reset the shake count.
                            if (ValidateInput(InputValue.Text))
                            {
                                double enteredNumber;
                                if (double.TryParse(InputValue.Text, out enteredNumber))
                                {
                                    double result = enteredNumber * enteredNumber;
                                    this.Dispatcher.BeginInvoke(() =>
                                    {
```

```
                        Operation.Text = InputValue.Text + " ^ 2 = ";
                        Result.Text = result.ToString();

                                                    this.Focus();
                    });
                }
                else
                {
                    this.Dispatcher.BeginInvoke(() =>
                    {
                        Operation.Text = "Please enter a valid number";
                    });
                }
            }
        }
        else if (DetectShakeMotion(_lastAccelerometerReading,
    currentAccelerometerReading, _shakeThreshold))
        {
            // Increment the shake count if this is the first part of
    the shake motion.
            _shakeCount++;
        }
        else if (!DetectShakeMotion(_lastAccelerometerReading,
    currentAccelerometerReading, 0.2))
        {
            // Reset the shake motion count and shaking motion flag if
    the shaking motion has stopped.
            _shakeCount = 0;
            _shaking = false;
        }
        // Save the current reading to compare with the next.
        _lastAccelerometerReading = currentAccelerometerReading;
    }
}
catch (Exception)
{
}
}
else
{
}
}
```

Two consecutive readings from the accelerometer are compared every time the ReadingChanged event handler is fired. If the difference in the value is more than a threshold value, we mark the event as a shake action. Subsequent ReadingChanged events are tracked to reset the shake motion count and the flag. The DetectShakeMotion method calculates the difference between the current and previous readings from the accelerometer and determines if the phone has been shaken:

```
private bool DetectShakeMotion(AccelerometerReadingEventArgs
        lastAccelerometerReading, AccelerometerReadingEventArgs
        currentAccelerometerReading, double threshold)
{
    double deltaX = Math.Abs((lastAccelerometerReading.X - currentAccelerom
        eterReading.X));
    double deltaY = Math.Abs((lastAccelerometerReading.Y - currentAccelerom
        eterReading.Y));
    double deltaZ = Math.Abs((lastAccelerometerReading.Z - currentAccelerom
        eterReading.Z));

    return (deltaX > threshold && deltaY > threshold) || (deltaX >
        threshold && deltaZ > threshold) || (deltaY > threshold && deltaZ
        > threshold);
}
```

Testing the App on a Windows Phone

The SwipeNShakeCalc application (shown in Figure 9-6) uses the accelerometer for detecting shake motion. So, you'll want to test it on a real Windows Phone device. In Chapter 16, we describe the process for putting an application out in the Marketplace so that you can test it.

Figure 9-6: The completed SwipeNShake
Calc application.

10

Cloudy Computing: Creating a Simple App to Go to the Internet

In This Chapter

▶ Understanding how to connect to the Internet and download data

▶ Designing an interface to display a list of items

▶ Using the web browser to open a page on the Internet

*W*indows Phones provide people ready connectivity to the Internet, through either the mobile network or a wireless network. Applications that use the Internet connectivity in a Windows Phone turn it into a gadget that's very handy for consuming information.

In this chapter, we build an application called Formula1News, which downloads news items on Formula 1 racing and displays them in a list. Tapping an individual item in a list opens the news item in a separate window. We show you how to display items in a list and use a web browser control in a separate page to display the news item selected from the list.

PhotoDisc, Inc.

Getting Your New App on the Net

In conventional applications, you may use sockets or high-level APIs to connect to the Internet. The Windows Phone 7 API provides two classes to connect your application to the Internet. These classes — `WebClient` and `HttpWebRequest` — are available in the `System.Net` namespace. You need to choose one of the two classes in your application to connect to the Internet and download data.

A very important difference exists between the two classes: When you use the `WebClient` class, the callback that delivers the data for the download request runs in the same thread that is used to update the user interface elements (that is, the user interface thread). However, a request to download data using the `HttpWebRequest` class runs on the application's main thread and leaves the user interface thread free. The callback to deliver the data must use a special way to update the user interface in order to avoid cross-thread exceptions.

In the following example, a new web request is created using the `WebClient` class. The result is delivered in the same thread, and the user interface is updated with the result:

```
private void DownloadWithWebClient()
{
    var webClient = new WebClient();

    webClient.OpenReadAsync(new Uri("http://www.msn.com"));
    webClient.OpenReadCompleted += new OpenReadCompletedEventHandler(webCli
        ent_OpenReadCompleted);

}

void webClient_OpenReadCompleted(object sender, OpenReadCompletedEventArgs
        e)
{

    using (var reader = new StreamReader(e.Result))
    {
        Result.Text = reader.ReadToEnd();
    }
}
```

When using the `HttpWebRequest` class, the response from the request to download data runs on a separate thread. In order to update the user interface with the result, the user interface thread must be used. Here is the code that demonstrates the use of the `HttpWebRequest` class:

```
private void DownloadWithHttpWebRequest()
{
    string url = "http://www.msn.com";

    var request = HttpWebRequest.Create(url);
    var result = (IAsyncResult)request.BeginGetResponse(HttpWebRequestRespo
        nseCallback, request);
}

private void HttpWebRequestResponseCallback(IAsyncResult result)
{
    var request = (HttpWebRequest)result.AsyncState;
    var response = request.EndGetResponse(result);

    using (var stream = response.GetResponseStream())
    using (var reader = new StreamReader(stream))
    {
```

```
        var contents = reader.ReadToEnd();
        // Deliver data to the user interface thread
        Dispatcher.BeginInvoke(() => { Result.Text = contents; });
    }
}
```

When developing Windows Phone apps that connect to the Internet and download data, remember that the `WebClient` class runs on the user interface thread, so the user interface is not responsive while data is being downloaded from the Internet. On the other hand, the `HttpWebRequest` class does not block the user interface thread, and your application is responsive. So, in apps where a large amount of data is to be downloaded from the Internet or if the source of the data is slow to access, you should use the `HttpWebRequest` class; in all other cases, you should use the `WebClient` class.

If you want to know more about the differences between the two classes, check out this thread on Stack Overflow: `http://bit.ly/jNCySj`.

Pulling information from the Internet

The app we build in this chapter has the following important features:

- ✔ It uses the `WebClient` class to download data from a RSS feed.

- ✔ It processes the data downloaded from the Internet and populates a ListBox with the data. A ListBox is a user interface element that is used to display a list of items in a page.

- ✔ It uses the `WebBrowser` control to display a news item from the URL present in each news item.

We use the RSS feed for the latest Formula 1 news available from the URL `www.formula1.com/rss/news/latest.rss`. An RSS feed is an XML document that can be parsed for each news item. A news item in the feed appears as follows:

```
<item>
<title>
Q&A with Red Bull's Sebastian Vettel
</title>
<description>
It was another imperious victory for 'Super Seb' Vettel in Turkey on Sunday. The
            world champion is not keen on such nicknames, but even he had to
            admit that 'super' was a pretty apt description of his race. The
            German insists he is not thinking about the title yet, instead
            following his father's advice to take it one step at a time -
            advice that served him very well last season...
</description>
<link>
http://www.formula1.com/news/interviews/2011/5/12014.html
</link>
```

(continued)

(continued)

```
<pubDate>
Sun, 08 May 2011 17:22:00 GMT
</pubDate>
<guid isPermaLink="true">
http://www.formula1.com/news/interviews/2011/5/12014.html
</guid>
<source url="http://www.formula1.com">
Formula1.com
</source>
</item>
```

In the list that displays the news item, we use the data from the `title`, `description`, and `pubDate` fields. We also use the `link` field to wire up a page that is opened with the URL when the user taps a news item.

Reformatting it for the small screen

The data available in the news feed needs to be formatted such that it fits in the small screen of a Windows Phone. We arrange the data in a ListBox, with each item in the ListBox showing the title, description, and publication date of the news item. Figure 10-1 is a single news item from the completed app.

Every item in a ListBox is formatted according to a template called a DataTemplate. A DataTemplate defines the layout of each item in the ListBox. Individual user interface elements in a DataTemplate are bound to the properties of an object; a ListBox is bound to a collection of objects. When the RSS feed is downloaded and parsed by the application, a collection of objects is created with each object representing a news item.

In the following sections, we tell you how to build the app and test it on a device.

Figure 10-1: A single news item displayed in the Formula1News app.

Get Ready: Planning the User's Experience of Your App

In the previous section, we tell you how to obtain the RSS feed from the Formula 1 website and introduce you to the design of the application. In this section, we build the user interface, write the code to download the RSS feed and use it in the application, and test it.

Building the user interface

Follow these steps to create your new project in Visual Studio:

1. **Open Visual Studio, and select File⇨New⇨Project.**

   The New Project dialog box appears.

2. **Click Silverlight for Windows Phone in the left column and then select the Windows Phone Databound Application template.**

3. **Name your project Formula1News (see Figure 10-2).**

Figure 10-2: Create a new project for Formula1News.

When you create a Databound application project for Windows Phone, the project template creates two XAML pages, `MainPage.xaml` and `DetailsPage.xaml`, along with two view model classes, `ItemViewModel` and `MainViewModel`. The view models provide the data that is displayed by the user interface elements.

In the app we're building, the `MainViewModel` class provides a collection of objects of the `ItemViewModel` class, each of which is bound to an item in the ListBox. Open `MainPage.xaml`, and modify the XAML to match the following:

```
<phone:PhoneApplicationPage
    x:Class="Formula1News.MainPage"
    xmlns="http://schemas.microsoft.com/winfx/2006/xaml/presentation"
    xmlns:x="http://schemas.microsoft.com/winfx/2006/xaml"
    xmlns:phone="clr-namespace:Microsoft.Phone.Controls;assembly=Microsoft.
        Phone"
    xmlns:shell="clr-namespace:Microsoft.Phone.Shell;assembly=Microsoft.Phone"
    xmlns:d="http://schemas.microsoft.com/expression/blend/2008"
    xmlns:mc="http://schemas.openxmlformats.org/markup-compatibility/2006"
    mc:Ignorable="d" d:DesignWidth="480" d:DesignHeight="768"
    d:DataContext="{d:DesignData SampleData/MainViewModelSampleData.xaml}"
    FontFamily="{StaticResource PhoneFontFamilyNormal}"
    FontSize="{StaticResource PhoneFontSizeNormal}"
    Foreground="{StaticResource PhoneForegroundBrush}"
    SupportedOrientations="Portrait"  Orientation="Portrait"
    shell:SystemTray.IsVisible="True">

    <!--Data context is set to sample data above and LayoutRoot contains the root
            Grid where all other page content is placed-->
    <Grid x:Name="LayoutRoot" Background="Transparent">
        <Grid.RowDefinitions>
            <RowDefinition Height="Auto"/>
            <RowDefinition Height="*"/>
        </Grid.RowDefinitions>

        <!--TitlePanel contains the name of the application and page title-->
        <StackPanel x:Name="TitlePanel" Grid.Row="0" Margin="12,17,0,28">
            <TextBlock x:Name="ApplicationTitle" Text="FORMULA 1 NEWS"
                Style="{StaticResource PhoneTextNormalStyle}"/>
        </StackPanel>

        <!--ContentPanel contains ListBox and ListBox ItemTemplate. Place
            additional content here-->
        <Grid x:Name="ContentPanel" Grid.Row="1" Margin="12,0,12,0">
            <ListBox x:Name="MainListBox" Margin="0,0,-12,0" ItemsSource="{Binding
                Items}" SelectionChanged="MainListBox_SelectionChanged">
                <ListBox.ItemTemplate>
                    <DataTemplate>
                        <Grid x:Name="NewsItemGrid" Width="405" Margin="0,15,0,0">
                            <Grid.RowDefinitions>
```

```
                                <RowDefinition Height="*" />
                                <RowDefinition Height="Auto" />
                                <RowDefinition Height="*" />
                                <RowDefinition Height="*" />
                        </Grid.RowDefinitions>
                        <Path Data="M0,0 L420,0" Stretch="Fill"
            UseLayoutRounding="False" Margin="0,2" Grid.ColumnSpan="1"
            VerticalAlignment="Bottom"
                        Stroke="{StaticResource PhoneAccentBrush}" Grid.Row="0"
            StrokeThickness="3"/>
                        <TextBlock x:Name="NewsItemTitle" Text="{Binding LineOne}"
            Grid.Row="1" HorizontalAlignment="Left" Margin="0" Padding="0"
            TextWrapping="Wrap" FontFamily="Segoe WP SemiLight" FontSize="32"
            Foreground="{StaticResource PhoneForegroundBrush}" />
                        <TextBlock x:Name="Description" Text="{Binding LineThree}"
            Grid.Row="2" Foreground="{StaticResource PhoneSubtleBrush}"
            TextWrapping="Wrap" FontFamily="Segoe WP SemiLight"
            FontSize="22"/>
                        <TextBlock x:Name="PublicationDate" Text="{Binding
            LineTwo}" Foreground="{StaticResource PhoneAccentBrush}" Grid.
            Row="3" FontSize="18" FontFamily="Segoe WP SemiLight" />
                    </Grid>
                </DataTemplate>
            </ListBox.ItemTemplate>
        </ListBox>
    </Grid>
  </Grid>

</phone:PhoneApplicationPage>
```

Note that the XAML for the ListBox DataTemplate consists of a Grid within which a path and three TextBlocks are present. Each TextBlock is bound to a property of the `ItemViewModel` class. Next, open the `ItemViewModel` class, and add the following code for a new property:

```
        private string _url;
        /// <summary>
        /// Sample ViewModel property; this property is used in the view to
                display its value using a Binding.
        /// </summary>
        /// <returns></returns>
        public string Url
        {
            get
            {
                return _url;
            }
            set
            {
```

(continued)

(continued)

```
            if (value != _url)
            {
                _url = value;
                NotifyPropertyChanged("Url");
            }
        }
    }
```

This new property is used to store the URL of the news item from the feed processed by the application. This property is used to open the news item in the next page of the app. Now that you have the first page of the app completed, open the `DetailsPage.xaml` file, and modify the XAML as follows:

```
<phone:PhoneApplicationPage
    x:Class="Formula1News.DetailsPage"
    xmlns="http://schemas.microsoft.com/winfx/2006/xaml/presentation"
    xmlns:x="http://schemas.microsoft.com/winfx/2006/xaml"
    xmlns:phone="clr-namespace:Microsoft.Phone.Controls;assembly=Microsoft.
            Phone"
    xmlns:shell="clr-namespace:Microsoft.Phone.Shell;assembly=Microsoft.Phone"
    xmlns:d="http://schemas.microsoft.com/expression/blend/2008"
    xmlns:mc="http://schemas.openxmlformats.org/markup-compatibility/2006"
    d:DataContext="{d:DesignData SampleData/MainViewModelSampleData.xaml}"
    mc:Ignorable="d" d:DesignWidth="480" d:DesignHeight="768"
    FontFamily="{StaticResource PhoneFontFamilyNormal}"
    FontSize="{StaticResource PhoneFontSizeNormal}"
    Foreground="{StaticResource PhoneForegroundBrush}"
    SupportedOrientations="Portrait"  Orientation="Portrait"
    shell:SystemTray.IsVisible="True">

    <!--Data context is set to sample data above and first item in sample data
            collection below and LayoutRoot contains the root Grid where all
            other page content is placed-->
    <Grid x:Name="LayoutRoot" Background="Transparent" d:DataContext="{Binding
            Items[0]}">
        <Grid.RowDefinitions>
            <RowDefinition Height="Auto"/>
            <RowDefinition Height="*"/>
        </Grid.RowDefinitions>

        <TextBlock x:Name="PageTitle" Text="FORMULA 1 NEWS"
                Style="{StaticResource PhoneTextNormalStyle}" Grid.Row="0"/>
        <phone:WebBrowser Name="webBrowser" Grid.Row="1" />
    </Grid>

</phone:PhoneApplicationPage>
```

You've added a `WebBrowser` control in the page. This control is used to display the web page from the URL present in each news item in the RSS feed.

Dealing with an HTTP request

You may have noticed that the ListBox in the main page is databound to a collection of items, `ItemsSource="{Binding Items}"`. This collection of items is provided through the data context of the underlying class, `MainPage`. An instance of the `MainViewModel` class is created when the application is created. The `LoadData` method of the `MainViewModel` class is where the RSS feed will be downloaded and parsed and the collection of objects will be databound to the ListBox.

The RSS feed downloaded from the URL is an XML document. We'll use the LINQ to XML API to parse the downloaded XML. So, add a reference to the `System.Xml.Linq` assembly, as shown in Figure 10-3.

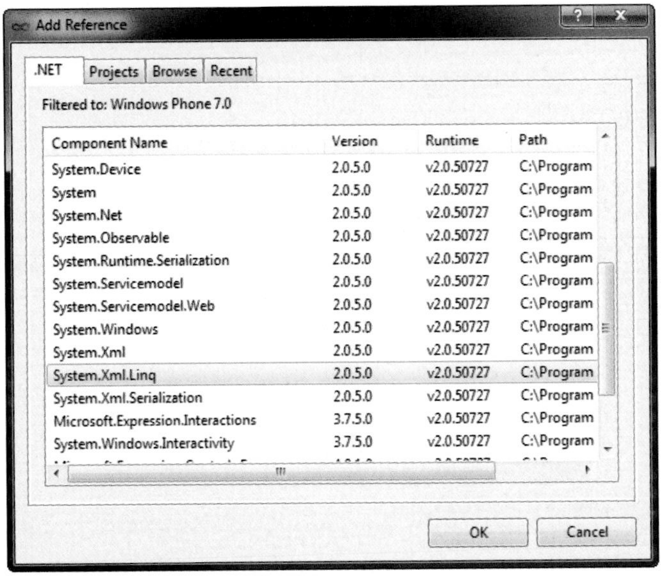

Figure 10-3: Add the `System.Xml.Linq` assembly to the project.

Next, open the `MainViewModel` class file, and add the following namespace imports:

```
// Namespace imports for application
using System.Net;
using System.IO;
using System.Linq;
using System.Xml.Linq;
```

Locate the `LoadData` method in the `MainViewModel` class, remove the existing code, and update the method with the following:

```
/// <summary>
/// Creates and adds a few ItemViewModel objects into the Items collection.
/// </summary>
public void LoadData()
{
    // Load the RSS feed items from the news Url
    string url = "http://www.formula1.com/rss/news/latest.rss";
    WebClient webClient = new WebClient();
    webClient.OpenReadCompleted += (sender, e) =>
    {
        if (e.Error != null)
            return;

        Stream str = e.Result;
        XDocument xdoc = XDocument.Load(str);

        // take 10 first results
        List<ItemViewModel> rssFeedItems = (from item in xdoc.
            Descendants("item")
                                            select new ItemViewModel()
                                            {
                                                LineOne = item.Element("title").
        Value,
                                                LineThree = item.
        Element("description").Value,
                                                Url = item.Element("link").
        Value,
                                                LineTwo = item.
        Element("pubDate").Value
                                            }).ToList();
        // close
        str.Close();

        // add results to listbox
        this.Items.Clear();
        foreach (ItemViewModel item in rssFeedItems)
        {
            this.Items.Add(item);
        }
    };
    webClient.OpenReadAsync(new Uri(url, UriKind.Absolute));
    this.IsDataLoaded = true;
}
```

We're using the WebClient class to download the RSS feed as an XML document, parsing it with the LINQ to XML API, creating an object of the ItemViewModel class for each item in the RSS feed, and binding to the ListBox through the collection of items. If you compile the code and run the application, you'll see the ListBox populated with data, as shown in Figure 10-4.

Figure 10-4: The completed main page of the Formula1News app.

You can scroll up and down through the list and read the summary of each news item. When a news item is tapped, the application should display the news item in a web browser in a new page. In the following section, we update the app to include this feature.

Using the WebBrowser control

The WebBrowser control can be used to open a web page on the Internet. You need to provide a valid URL and call the Navigate method. Open the DetailsPage class, remove the OnNavigatedTo method, and add the following method:

```
// When page is loaded to set data context to selected item in list
void DetailsPage_Loaded(object sender, RoutedEventArgs e)
{
    string selectedIndex = "";
    if (NavigationContext.QueryString.TryGetValue("selectedItem", out
        selectedIndex))
```

(continued)

(continued)

```
    {
        int index = int.Parse(selectedIndex);
        string url = App.ViewModel.Items[index].Url;
        webBrowser.Navigate(new Uri(url));
    }
}
```

This method is the event handler for the `Loaded` event. We need to wire up this event handler with the `Loaded` event of the `DetailsPage` class. Update the `DetailsPage` class constructor as follows:

```
// Constructor
public DetailsPage()
{
    InitializeComponent();
    this.Loaded += new RoutedEventHandler(DetailsPage_Loaded);
}
```

When a ListBox item in the main page is tapped, the following event handler is invoked:

```
// Handle selection changed on ListBox
private void MainListBox_SelectionChanged(object sender,
        SelectionChangedEventArgs e)
{
    // If selected index is -1 (no selection) do nothing
    if (MainListBox.SelectedIndex == -1)
        return;

    // Navigate to the new page
    NavigationService.Navigate(new Uri("/DetailsPage.xaml?selectedItem=" +
            MainListBox.SelectedIndex, UriKind.Relative));

    // Reset selected index to -1 (no selection)
    MainListBox.SelectedIndex = -1;
}
```

Note that the selected items' index in the collection of items is passed into the details page. In the `DetailsPage_Loaded` method, this index is used to access the object and its `Url` property. The URL of the news item is used with the `WebBrowser` control to open the news page for the news item. Figure 10-5 shows the page of the application with the `WebBrowser` control displaying the news page.

Figure 10-5: The completed details page of the Formula1News app.

Making the App Perform to Your Standards

The app you've built in this chapter can be tested entirely with the Windows Phone Emulator. However, testing the app on a real Windows Phone is always a good idea. After thoroughly testing it with the emulator, prepare the XAP file, and use Windows Phone Application Deployment to deploy the application to the phone to test it.

The app you've built is simple and doesn't require any configuration or setup to view Formula 1 news. You may consider an enhancement of the app in which a new page is added to configure additional news feed sources, the user is allowed to mark a news item as read so that it isn't shown in the future, and so on. For the purposes of this chapter, the features we've built in the Formula1News app are sufficient.

We walk you through the submission process in Chapter 16.

11

I Can Hear You Now: A Simple Multimedia App

In This Chapter

▶ Writing an app that uses the accelerometer

▶ Testing your app on an actual phone

*E*very Windows Phone device includes an FM radio. You can listen to an FM radio station by opening the Music + Videos hub on your Windows Phone and selecting the radio option from the list. Tune in to the radio station of your choice by swiping your finger on the slider control, either toward the left or toward the right.

Tuning to an FM radio station using the slider is fine, but you may want to change the station by shaking the phone. In this chapter, we show you how to build an app that will tune in to a new radio station when the phone is shaken.

Getting Acquainted with the App

The app we build in this chapter consists of the following important features:

Digital Vision

✔ The application will provide the user an interface to turn on or off the FM radio tuner with the click of a button.

✔ The app will let the user tune in to a new station when the phone is shaken.

✔ When the user exits the app, the frequency of the radio station will be saved in the app's settings.

✔ The user will be able to use the application bar in the app to play and pause the radio.

The application consists of a single page, with the tuned frequency displayed at the top, and an application bar with a play and a pause button. When the application starts, it tries to retrieve the last tuned frequency from the application's settings. It turns on the radio to the last tuned frequency (if it's obtained from the app's settings) or to a frequency at the beginning of the FM radio spectrum.

Note that the Windows Phone 7 FM tuner API provides `RadioRegion` enumeration that can have the value of Europe, Japan, or United States. In our application, we set the enumeration to United States before powering on the FM tuner. This restricts us to the frequency band 88.1 MHz to 107.9 MHz.

The user can then shake the phone to tune in to a new FM radio station by shaking the phone. The frequency is incremented in steps of 0.1 MHz. The application allows the user to power off the radio at the click of the pause button. Note that the buttons are enabled or disabled based on whether the FM tuner is turned on or off.

Writing the Code

In this section, we describe the steps you take to create the user interface of the app, write the code that provide the core features of the app, and get the app ready for testing.

Creating the Shake And Tune app for the FM radio

Follow these steps to create your new project in Visual Studio:

1. **Open Visual Studio, and select File⇨New⇨Project.**

   The New Project dialog box appears.

2. **Click Silverlight for Windows Phone in the left column and then select the Windows Phone Application template.**

3. **Name your project ShakeAndTune (see Figure 11-1).**

Add two icons to the project so that they can be used in the application bar:

1. **Right-click the project in the Solution Explorer, select Add, click New Folder, and name the new folder Images.**

2. **Copy PNG files of the two icons into the newly created folder.**

   You need two PNG files: one for the play button and the other for the pause button. You can download icons for the Metro theme from `http://metro.windowswiki.info` — you're free to use these icons in your apps. The icons also are installed on your machine when you install the Windows Phone SDK; they're located in `C:\Program Files\Microsoft SDKs\Windows Phone\v7.0\Icons`.

Microsoft suggests using black-and-white icons instead of color ones. When the user changes the theme in the phone to one with a white background, the icons are automatically reversed.

Figure 11-1: Create a new project for ShakeAndTune.

3. **Right-click the Images folder, and choose Add⇨Existing Item.**

   Now that you've added the two PNG files to your project, you must ensure that they are compiled and are available for use as icons in the application bar buttons.

4. **Right-click each image, and select Properties.**

   The Properties pane opens.

5. **For the Build Action property, select Content (see Figure 11-2), change the Copy to Output Property value to Copy If Newer, and save the project.**

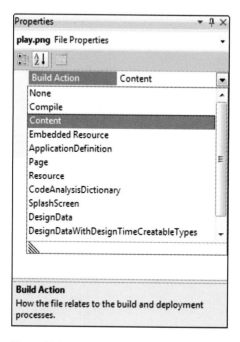

Figure 11-2: Change the build action of the PNG files.

Now that you have the required resources added to the project, open the `MainPage.xaml` file in Visual Studio. Update the `ApplicationTitle` TextBlock's Text property to `SHAKE AND TUNE` (or any other name you might have chosen). We'll use the `PageTitle` TextBlock to display the frequency of the currently tuned FM radio station. And we'll use a system style `PhoneTextHugeStyle` in the `PageTitle` TextBlock.

You can view a list of system styles available in Windows Phone 7 applications at `http://bit.ly/dByZDj`.

When you create a new Windows Phone 7 app, you'll find that the application bar XAML is commented out in the `MainPage.xaml` file. In our application, we'll use the application bar. Uncomment the section of XAML that declares it, and make the changes in the XAML as shown here. The XAML of the whole page looks like this:

```
<phone:PhoneApplicationPage
    x:Class="ShakeAndTune.MainPage"
    xmlns="http://schemas.microsoft.com/winfx/2006/xaml/presentation"
    xmlns:x="http://schemas.microsoft.com/winfx/2006/xaml"
    xmlns:phone="clr-namespace:Microsoft.Phone.Controls;assembly=Microsoft.
        Phone"
```

```xml
    xmlns:shell="clr-namespace:Microsoft.Phone.Shell;assembly=Microsoft.Phone"
    xmlns:d="http://schemas.microsoft.com/expression/blend/2008"
    xmlns:mc="http://schemas.openxmlformats.org/markup-compatibility/2006"
    mc:Ignorable="d" d:DesignWidth="480" d:DesignHeight="696"
    FontFamily="{StaticResource PhoneFontFamilyNormal}"
    FontSize="{StaticResource PhoneFontSizeNormal}"
    Foreground="{StaticResource PhoneForegroundBrush}"
    SupportedOrientations="Portrait" Orientation="Portrait"
    shell:SystemTray.IsVisible="True">

<!--LayoutRoot is the root Grid where all page content is placed-->
<Grid x:Name="LayoutRoot" Background="Transparent">
    <Grid.RowDefinitions>
        <RowDefinition Height="Auto"/>
        <RowDefinition Height="*"/>
    </Grid.RowDefinitions>

    <!--TitlePanel contains the name of the application and page title-->
    <StackPanel x:Name="TitlePanel" Grid.Row="0" Margin="12,17,0,28">
        <TextBlock x:Name="ApplicationTitle" Text="SHAKE AND TUNE"
                Style="{StaticResource PhoneTextNormalStyle}"/>
        <TextBlock x:Name="PageTitle" Text="" Margin="9,-7,0,0"
                Style="{StaticResource PhoneTextHugeStyle}"/>
    </StackPanel>

    <!--ContentPanel - place additional content here-->
    <Grid x:Name="ContentPanel" Grid.Row="1" Margin="12,0,12,0"></Grid>
</Grid>

<!--Sample code showing usage of ApplicationBar-->
<phone:PhoneApplicationPage.ApplicationBar>
    <shell:ApplicationBar IsVisible="True" IsMenuEnabled="True">
        <shell:ApplicationBarIconButton x:Name="playButton"
                                        IconUri="/Images/play.png"
                                        Text="Play"
                                        Click="Play_Click"/>
        <shell:ApplicationBarIconButton x:Name="pauseButton"
                                        IconUri="/Images/pause.png"
                                        Text="Pause"
                                        Click="Pause_Click"
                                        IsEnabled="False"/>
    </shell:ApplicationBar>
</phone:PhoneApplicationPage.ApplicationBar>

</phone:PhoneApplicationPage>
```

Notice that in our application, we won't be using the `ContentPanel` Grid. You may keep the Grid in the XAML shown above without any issues.

Soon, we'll add code to turn on and off the radio in these event handlers.

Using the accelerometer for shake detection

A fundamental feature of the application is the ability to detect shake motion and change the frequency of the FM radio station. We'll use the accelerometer in the Windows Phone to detect any shake motion of the device. In order to develop the code to detect the shake motion, we have to add a reference to the `Microsoft.Devices.Sensors` assembly:

1. **Right-click the project, and select Add Reference.**

   The Add Reference dialog box opens.

2. **Select the `Microsoft.Devices.Sensors` assembly (see Figure 11-3), and click OK.**

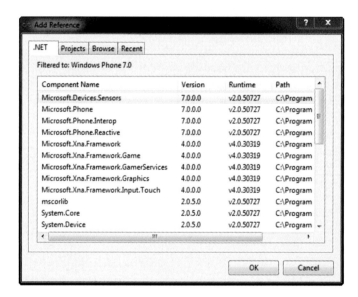

Figure 11-3: Add the `Microsoft.Devices.Sensors` assembly to the project

3. **Add the following namespace directives in the `MainPage.xaml.cs` file:**

```
// Namespace imports for application
using System.IO.IsolatedStorage;
using Microsoft.Devices.Radio;
using Microsoft.Devices.Sensors;
using Microsoft.Phone.Shell;
```

In the constructor of the `MainPage` class, we need to set up the FM tuner and the accelerometer for the shake detection. Here is the code for the constructor:

```csharp
// Constructor
public MainPage()
{
    InitializeComponent();

    // Check if the last tuned FM radio station is stored in the
        application's settings. If present, set up the tuner with it.
    double frequency = 88.1;
    string lastTunedStation = string.Empty;
    IsolatedStorageSettings.ApplicationSettings.TryGetValue<string>("l
        astTunedStation", out lastTunedStation);
    if (!string.IsNullOrEmpty(lastTunedStation))
    {
        bool conversionResult = double.TryParse(lastTunedStation, out
        frequency);
    }

    try
    {
        FMRadio fmRadio = FMRadio.Instance;
        fmRadio.CurrentRegion = RadioRegion.UnitedStates;
        fmRadio.PowerMode = RadioPowerMode.On;
        fmRadio.Frequency = frequency;
        _currentFrequency = frequency;
    }
    catch (Exception ex)
    {
        MessageBox.Show(ex.ToString());
    }
    finally
    {
        // Update the display
        PageTitle.Text = string.Format("{0:0.0}", _currentFrequency);

        // Disable the play button and enable the pause button
        playButton = (ApplicationBarIconButton)this.ApplicationBar.
        Buttons[0];
        playButton.IsEnabled = false;

        pauseButton = (ApplicationBarIconButton)this.ApplicationBar.
        Buttons[1];
        pauseButton.IsEnabled = true;
    }

    // Set up the accelerometer for shake detection.
    _accelerometer = new Accelerometer();
    _accelerometer.ReadingChanged += new EventHandler<AccelerometerRea
        dingEventArgs>(Accelerometer_ReadingChanged);
    _accelerometer.Start();
}
```

Note that the application tries to retrieve the last tuned FM radio station from the application's settings. In any application, if you want to store a few settings between restarts of the app, you should use `ApplicationSettings` with a key. Alternatively, if you need to store large amounts of data, such as a file downloaded by the application, you should use `IsolatedStorageFile`. Jeff Blankenburg has a concise article discussing the two classes at `http://bit.ly/11R21U`.

Next, we have to set up the accelerometer by connecting an event handler for the `ReadingChanged` event. This event is fired every time there is change in the readings provided by the phone's accelerometer. We'll use the current readings from the accelerometer and compare it with the previous reading to detect if the phone has been shaken by the user. If the phone is shaken, the frequency of the FM tuner is incremented by 0.1 MHz. Here's the code of the `ReadingChanged` event handler:

```
void Accelerometer_ReadingChanged(object sender,
        AccelerometerReadingEventArgs e)
{
    if (_accelerometer.State == SensorState.Ready)
    {
        AccelerometerReadingEventArgs currentAccelerometerReading = e;
        try
        {
            if (_lastAccelerometerReading != null) // We can now check if the
            phone was shaken by the user
            {
                if (!_shaking && DetectShakeMotion(_lastAccelerometerReading,
                currentAccelerometerReading, _shakeThreshold) && _shakeCount >= 1)
                {

                    // Update frequency and check for upper bound
                    _currentFrequency = _currentFrequency + _frequencyIncrement;
                    if (_currentFrequency >= 107.9)
                        _currentFrequency = 88.1;

                    // Shaking motion detected, retune frequency
                    FMRadio fmRadio = FMRadio.Instance;
                    fmRadio.Frequency = _currentFrequency;
                    this.Dispatcher.BeginInvoke(() =>
                    {
                        // Update the display
                        PageTitle.Text = string.Format("{0:0.0}", _
                    currentFrequency);
                    });
                }
                else if (DetectShakeMotion(_lastAccelerometerReading,
                currentAccelerometerReading, _shakeThreshold))
                {
```

```
                // Increment the shake count if this is the first part of
        the shake motion
                _shakeCount++;
            }
            else if (!DetectShakeMotion(_lastAccelerometerReading,
        currentAccelerometerReading, 0.2))
            {
                // Reset the shake motion count and shaking motion flag if
        the shaking motion has stopped
                _shakeCount = 0;
                _shaking = false;
            }
        }

        // Save the current reading to compare with the next
        _lastAccelerometerReading = currentAccelerometerReading;
    }
    catch
    {
    }
}
}
```

Two consecutive readings from the accelerometer are compared every time the ReadingChanged event handler is fired. If the difference in the value is more than a threshold value, we mark the event as a shake action. Subsequent ReadingChanged events are tracked to reset the shake motion count and the flag. Every time the FM tuner's frequency is changed, the current frequency is displayed in the application.

The DetectShakeMotion method calculates the difference between the current and previous readings from the accelerometer and determines if the phone has been shaken:

```
private bool DetectShakeMotion(AccelerometerReadingEventArgs
        lastAccelerometerReading, AccelerometerReadingEventArgs
        currentAccelerometerReading, double threshold)
{
    double deltaX = Math.Abs((lastAccelerometerReading.X - currentAccelerom
        eterReading.X));
    double deltaY = Math.Abs((lastAccelerometerReading.Y - currentAccelerom
        eterReading.Y));
    double deltaZ = Math.Abs((lastAccelerometerReading.Z - currentAccelerom
        eterReading.Z));

    return (deltaX > threshold && deltaY > threshold) || (deltaX >
        threshold && deltaZ > threshold) || (deltaY > threshold && deltaZ
        > threshold);
}
```

Before we proceed to the hook up the event handlers for the play and pause buttons, we need to add some variables for the MainPage class in the `MainPage.xaml.cs` file:

```
private double _currentFrequency = 88.1;
public double CurrentFrequency
{
   get
   {
      return _currentFrequency;
   }
   set
   {
      _currentFrequency = value;
   }
}
private double _frequencyIncrement = 0.1;
private const double _shakeThreshold = 0.5;
private Accelerometer _accelerometer;
private AccelerometerReadingEventArgs _lastAccelerometerReading;
private bool _shaking;
private int _shakeCount;
```

Wiring up the play and pause buttons

When the application starts, the FM tuner is set to either the last tuned frequency or the frequency at the beginning of the FM frequency band. The application should provide the user the ability to power on or power off the FM tuner. We'll use the application bar buttons and the associated event handlers to provide the user these features.

Add the following event handlers to the `MainPage` class in the `MainPage.xaml.cs` file:

```
/// <summary>
/// Power on the radio and tune into the current frequency
/// </summary>
/// <param name="sender"></param>
/// <param name="e"></param>
private void Play_Click(object sender, EventArgs e)
{
    FMRadio fmRadio = FMRadio.Instance;
    fmRadio.CurrentRegion = RadioRegion.UnitedStates;
    fmRadio.PowerMode = RadioPowerMode.On;
    fmRadio.Frequency = _currentFrequency;
```

```
    // Update the display
    PageTitle.Text = string.Format("{0:0.0}", _currentFrequency);

    // Disable the play button and enable the pause button
    playButton = (ApplicationBarIconButton)this.ApplicationBar.Buttons[0];
    playButton.IsEnabled = false;

    pauseButton = (ApplicationBarIconButton)this.ApplicationBar.Buttons[1];
    pauseButton.IsEnabled = true;
}

/// <summary>
/// Power off the radio
/// </summary>
/// <param name="sender"></param>
/// <param name="e"></param>
private void Pause_Click(object sender, EventArgs e)
{
    FMRadio fmRadio = FMRadio.Instance;
    fmRadio.PowerMode = RadioPowerMode.Off;

    // Disable the play button and enable the pause button
    playButton = (ApplicationBarIconButton)this.ApplicationBar.Buttons[0];
    playButton.IsEnabled = true;

    pauseButton = (ApplicationBarIconButton)this.ApplicationBar.Buttons[1];
    pauseButton.IsEnabled = false;
}
```

Notice that the buttons are enabled and disabled based on the state of the FM tuner. If the FM tuner is powered on, the play button is disabled and the pause button is enabled. It's the other way around if the FM tuner is powered off.

Saving the last tuned FM station

The application may be shut down by the user, or it may go in the background when a phone call is received by the phone. In such cases, it's ideal for the application to save the last tuned FM frequency in the application's settings.

In the core application class file (App.xaml.cs), we'll add a method, SaveLastTunedFrequency, that obtains the running instance of the MainPage class and stores the current frequency in the application's settings. This method is then called in both the Application_Deactivated and Application_Closing events:

```
// Code to execute when the application is deactivated (sent to background)
// This code will not execute when the application is closing
private void Application_Deactivated(object sender, DeactivatedEventArgs
        e)
{
    SaveLastTunedFrequency();
}

// Code to execute when the application is closing (eg, user hit Back)
// This code will not execute when the application is deactivated
private void Application_Closing(object sender, ClosingEventArgs e)
{
    SaveLastTunedFrequency();
}

private void SaveLastTunedFrequency()
{
    MainPage mainPage = ((App)Application.Current).RootFrame.Content as
        MainPage;
    if (mainPage != null) // Save the current frequency
    {
        double currentFrequency = mainPage.CurrentFrequency;
        if (IsolatedStorageSettings.ApplicationSettings.
          Contains("lastTunedStation"))
        {
            IsolatedStorageSettings.ApplicationSettings["lastTunedStation"] =
            currentFrequency;
        }
        else
        {
            IsolatedStorageSettings.ApplicationSettings.
            Add("lastTunedStation", currentFrequency);
        }
    }
}
```

After adding the preceding code, add the following namespace declaration at the top of the App.xaml.cs file:

```
// Namespace imports for application
using System.IO.IsolatedStorage;
```

The completed application is shown in Figure 11-4.

Figure 11-4: The completed
ShakeAndTune application.

Testing the App on a Windows Phone

In this application, we're using the FM tuner and the accelerometer. These
are hardware sensors, so you'll want to test on a real Windows Phone device
rather than relying on the emulator before finalizing your application and getting it ready for the Marketplace. This idea was first presented in Chapter 5.
In many cases, such as the previous two apps, testing on the device emulator
is sufficient.

When you acquire a Windows Phone to test on, you'll need to remember the
following points:

✔ **You need to disconnect your phone from the PC used for development.** Debugging is possible if you use the Windows Phone Connect Tool, but it's best to disconnect the phone from your PC and then test the app. (Sometimes, you may be at a location where the FM signal strength is very weak. You may want to move to a location in a room that has better FM reception. Plus, you'll find it convenient to test the shake-to-tune feature with the phone disconnected from your PC.)

Use the Deploy option instead of Debug in the project menu (right-click the project in the Solution Explorer to open the project menu).

✔ **Keep the earpiece connected when testing.** The FM tuner requires the earpiece to be connected because it uses the earpiece as an antenna.

We walk you through the submission process in Chapter 16.

Part IV
Getting Fancy with APIs

The 5th Wave   By Rich Tennant

HORNER BROS.
MAKERS OF PREMIUM
BELLS & WHISTLES

"As an application developer, I never thought I'd say this, but your app needs more bells and whistles."

In this part . . .

*N*ow that you've written some basic apps, Part IV adds the dimension of using some of the application programmer interfaces (APIs) provided by Microsoft. Using these APIs gives you experience in controlling resources on the phone.

Ultimately, every application — from the most basic to the most complicated — is about taking user input and interacting with APIs. After you master using the APIs presented in this chapter, you'll have the tools you need to control any resource that Microsoft makes available on Windows Phone 7.

Photo credits: Artville/Getty Images (top); PhotoDisc/Getty Images (middle); PhotoDisc, Inc. (bottom)

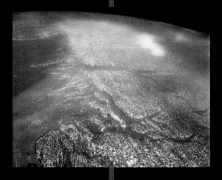

Pushing on the Accelerometer

*T*he accelerometer in the Windows Phone responds to movements and measures the device's motion in space along the *x*-axis, *y*-axis, and *z*-axis. The movement is measured with reference to the Earth's gravitational pull, which is downward (toward the Earth's center).

You can add simple yet interesting effects in your application by using the data obtained from the phone's accelerometer. For example, using the accelerometer, your app could generate a random number or choose a picture from the Pictures hub when the user shakes the phone. As the user moves the phone like a sword, your app could vary the pitch of the music being played on the phone.

The accelerometer is accessible through the standard Windows Phone API in both Silverlight and XNA applications. Because all Windows Phones have an accelerometer, you may use the accelerometer to introduce some fancy effects in your application. The only limit is your imagination.

In this chapter, you discover how to use the information from the accelerometer in applications that respond to the phone's movement. Turn to Chapter 14 for more on using the accelerometer in applications that respond to changes in the phone's orientation (that is, from portrait to landscape and vice versa).

Flat Earth

Knowing What the Accelerometer Tells You

When you hold your Windows Phone, the three axes point along the length of the phone (the y-axis), along the width of the phone (the x-axis), and perpendicular to the body of the phone (the z-axis), as shown in Figure 12-1.

Figure 12-1: The three axes of the accelerometer in the Windows Phone.

When the phone is not moving at all, the values of the accelerometer will be +1 or –1, depending on the orientation of the phone. As you move the phone, this value will change and lie between –2 and +2 in gravitational units.

The phone's orientation determines the value of the reading from the accelerometer. You can use these values in your application to update the background color of the page, start or stop an animation, and so on. Rotating the phone will tell you the current value of the accelerometer.

Here are three different scenarios in which the phone's accelerometer readings change:

- **Holding the phone upright:** When you're holding the phone facing toward you, the value of the accelerometer reading is (0,–1,0). This value tells you that the phone is pointing down. If you rotate the phone by 180 degrees such that the controls are pointing opposite to the previous position (meaning, the phone is upside down), the accelerometer reading will be (0,1,0).

- **Rotating the phone left or right:** If you rotate the phone by 90 degrees with the phone's controls toward the right, the value from the accelerometer changes to (–1,0,0). If you rotate the phone by 90 degrees with the phone's controls toward the left, the accelerometer will have a value of (1,0,0).

- **Laying the phone flat:** If you lay the phone down on a flat surface with the screen facing you, the accelerometer will read (0,0,–1). When you place the phone flat on the table with its face on the table, the accelerometer will read (0,0,1).

You can use the phone's orientation (landscape versus portrait) in your application to change the page layout and present a different layout that is suitable for the current orientation. (We show you how to use the phone's orientation in your application in Chapter 14.)

Working with the Phone's Accelerometer

In order to use the accelerometer data from the Windows Phone in your application, you need to add a reference to `Microsoft.Devices.Sensors` assembly and the `using Microsoft.Devices.Sensors` directive in your code. The namespace contains the `Accelerometer` class, which provides your application the ability to access the accelerometer API. The `Accelerometer` class is used to start, stop, and retrieve the values of the *x*-axis, *y*-axis, and *z*-axis, as well as the time.

You'll first create an `Accelerometer` object and subscribe to the `ReadingChanged` event. Then you'll call `Start` on the `Accelerometer` object.

```
using Microsoft.Devices.Sensors;

        Accelerometer acc = new Accelerometer();

        acc.ReadingChanged += new EventHandler<AccelerometerReadingEventArgs
           >(Accelerometer_ReadingChanged);
        try
        {
            acc.Start();
        }
        catch (AccelerometerFailedException)
        {
            // Error starting the accelerometer.
        }
```

You'll use the `Accelerometer_ReadingChanged` event handler to access the accelerometer readings. The `AccelerometerReadingEventArgs` argument in the event handler contains a time stamp showing when the data was read by the accelerometer, as well as a set of *x*, *y*, and *z* values.

Note that the event handler doesn't run on the user interface thread. So, you must use the user interface thread to update the interface on the phone (such as a `Textblock`) with the values obtained from the accelerometer. The following code sample illustrates how to use the values from the accelerometer:

```
        void Accelerometer_ReadingChanged(object sender,
            AccelerometerReadingEventArgs e)
        {
            Deployment.Current.Dispatcher.BeginInvoke(() => AccelerometerReading
                Changed(e));
        }

        void MyReadingChanged(AccelerometerReadingEventArgs e)
        {
            xValueTextblock.Text = e.X.ToString("0.00");
            yValueTextblock.Text = e.Y.ToString("0.00");
            zValueTextblock.Text = e.Z.ToString("0.00");
            timeValueTextblock.Text = e.Timestamp.ToString();
        }
```

Before the application terminates, you should call `Stop` on the `Accelerometer` object. Note that calling `Stop` may give rise to an `AccelerometerFailedException` exception.

```
try
{
    acc.Stop();
}
catch (AccelerometerFailedException)
{
    // Error stopping the accelerometer.
}
```

The `Accelerometer` class provides the `State` property, which tells you the current state of the phone's accelerometer. The `State` property can have any one of the following values:

- **NotSupported:** The sensor hardware is unavailable in the device.

- **Ready:** The accelerometer is available and ready to provide data.

- **Initializing:** The accelerometer is available and currently being initialized.

- **NoData:** The accelerometer is unable to obtain data.

- **NoPermissions:** The application attempting to use accelerometer data does not have permission to access the data.

- **Disabled:** The accelerometer is disabled in the device.

Tricking the Emulator: Your PC in Motion

The Windows Phone Emulator doesn't have an accelerometer. So, when you run a simple application to display the *x*-axis, *y*-axis, and *z*-axis values, you'll always see a value of (0,0,–1). (You would see the same values in the application running on the phone if it were facing you.) The simple application that displays the raw accelerometer values is shown in Figure 12-2.

If you don't have a Windows Phone device on which to test your applications using the accelerometer, you need to be able to simulate the accelerometer and supply the values of the *x*-axis, *y*-axis, and *z*-axis as expected in the real device. You have a couple options:

- **The accelerometer Wii controller:** If you want to use a physical device connected to your PC while you're developing an application with the accelerometer, using a Wii connected to your PC is the best option. First, you need to set up your Wii controller with your PC through Bluetooth. Bill Reiss, a Microsoft Silverlight MVP, has written a blog post describing the setup of the Wii controller for accelerometer emulation; check it out at `http://bit.ly/b1SRrE`.

✔ **The Windows Phone 7 Accelerometer Simulator Kit:** Unlike the preceding option, the simulator kit uses a software application to provide accelerometer values to your application. This kit is available at CodePlex (`http://wp7accelerometerkit.codeplex.com`). You'll need to include a DLL in your application to test the accelerometer and remove it after your application is ready for testing on a real device.

✔ **Reactive extensions for .NET:** Reactive extensions allow LINQ expressions to be written against events. Reactive extensions are beyond the scope of this book. However, if you're interested in emulating the accelerometer in your application, refer to the MSDN resource article available at `http://bit.ly/gjm8mc`. A video that demonstrates how to use reactive extensions to emulate the accelerometer is available at `http://bit.ly/hj83m0`.

Figure 12-2: Values obtained from the accelerometer in the emulator.

You may want to switch between the Windows Phone Emulator and a real device while developing your application that utilizes the phone's accelerometer. Switching between the two is straightforward with the following code snippet:

```
if (Microsoft.Devices.Environment.DeviceType == DeviceType.Device)
{
    // We are reading x, y, and z values from the accelerometer in a
    real device.
}

else
{
    // We are reading x, y, and z values from the simulated
    accelerometer.
}
```

The alternative to this setup is to use a preprocessor directive WINDOWS_ PHONE and the following code snippet to switch between the simulated accelerometer and a real device:

```
#if WINDOWS_PHONE
// We are reading x, y, and z values from the accelerometer in a
    real device.
#else
// We are reading x, y, and z values from the simulated
    accelerometer.
#endif
```

Recognizing the Limits of the Accelerometer's Information

The accelerometer in Windows Phone provides data at the rate of 50 samples per second. You may want to use all this data in your application if you need your application to be very sensitive and react to the data. Some Windows Phone applications, such as a jukebox that picks a random song from the Music + Videos hub when the user shakes the phone, may not require the accelerometer data for more than one sample a second; other applications, such as an aircraft flight simulator, may require accelerometer data to be obtained several times a second. The number of times your application should use the accelerometer data in 1 second depends on the design of the application.

The Windows Phone team has published an article that provides guidance on using the accelerometer in Windows Phone 7: http://bit.ly/cXJ2EC. You can use the AccelerometerHelper class from the article in your application to filter and calibrate the data from the accelerometer.

Continuous use of the accelerometer will consume the battery of the phone. Turn off the accelerometer when it's no longer required by your application.

13

Directions to Location Services

In This Chapter

▶ Integrating location into your app

▶ Paying attention to privacy

*E*very Windows Phone ships with an assisted GPS (A-GPS) receiver. With A-GPS, the receiver uses cellphone towers or wireless networks, in addition to GPS satellites, to obtain the device's current location. This way of obtaining the device's location is somewhat less accurate than a GPS receiver that uses only satellites for positioning, but it's faster and more reliable. In addition, the A-GPS receiver consumes less battery power and works well indoors.

The Windows Phone API allows your application to easily access location data from the receiver. You'll obtain the current location of the device as the latitude and longitude. Then you can use this information to plot the location with the Bing Maps Silverlight control. Alternatively, you can query the Bing Maps web service to obtain the latitude and longitude of a street address.

You need to get permission from the user before accessing data from the location service. There is legitimate concern about the abuse of location information by stalkers and other malefactors. To prevent unintentional use of this information, all apps must get an okay from the user.

In some circumstances, location data may not be available. For example, users can disable the location service on their phones. There is also no location data when users aren't in the vicinity of cellphone towers, wireless networks, or GPS satellites. Your app should be designed to be able to function *without* available location data, or the app should warn users that it may not function properly if such data is unavailable.

Corbis Digital Stock

Even with A-GPS, the location service in a Windows Phone consumes battery power. So, it should be turned on when your application needs to obtain the current position and turned off as soon as the position is obtained and no longer needed. In applications that don't require high accuracy (for example, when an app needs to know only the city or the region where the device is located, not the precise address), you can use the low-accuracy setting of location services.

In this chapter, we fill you in on how to use location services in your app. We use the Bing Maps service to convert an address to a *geocode* (geographical coordinates, such as latitude and longitude) to plot it on the Bing Maps Silverlight control. We show you how to issue a reverse geocode request from your app to find the address of the location. And we introduce *geofencing,* a technique that indicates when a Windows Phone is moved outside a specified region.

If your app uses location services, you need a real device in order to test your app. The Windows Phone team has developed a Windows Phone GPS Emulator that you can download and use for testing your app with the Windows Phone Emulator or a real device. The article describing the Windows Phone GPS Emulator is available at `http://bit.ly/ey6q9X`. You may refer to the companion article posted on MSDN Channel 9 at `http://bit.ly/fmcNOx`.

After you've tested your app with the Windows Phone GPS Emulator, it's always wise to test it on a real hardware device using actual A-GPS data before submitting it to the Marketplace.

Getting Location Information into Your App

The Windows Phone API provides access to location services via the `GeoCoordinateWatcher` class. You'll need to add a reference to the `System.Device` assembly and the directive `using System.Device.Location` in your code. The `GeoCoordinateWatcher` class provides users a `PositionChanged` event. In the `PositionChanged` event, you'll obtain a `GeoCoordinate` object that contains the latitude and longitude of the location, altitude, horizontal and vertical accuracy, course, speed, and a flag that indicates whether the `GeoCoordinate` object contains valid values for latitude and longitude.

Geocoding

You can use the location service in two ways:

> ✔ **The location service can be started and allowed to run in the back-ground.** It will deliver location readings asynchronously through event handlers.
>
> ✔ **You can obtain location readings synchronously.** Your code will wait for the readings to be delivered.

The following code sample creates a GeoCoordinateWatcher instance and starts it asynchronously:

```
public void CoordinateWatcher_Start()
        {
            // Create a GeoCoordinateWatcher and specify the accuracy required.
            // Use GeoPositionAccuracy.Default unless high accuracy is required.
            GeoCoordinateWatcher watcher = new GeoCoordinateWatcher(GeoPositionA
                ccuracy.High);

            // Check if the user has provided permission to use the service.
            if (watcher.Permission == GeoPositionPermission.Denied)
            {
                // Permission to use location service denied by user.
}

            else
            {
                // Set movement threshold in meters. Use at least 30 to avoid
                numerous events generated by minor changes in the position of the
                device. Higher values also help to maximize battery life for the
                device.
watcher.MovementThreshold = 30;

                // Add handlers for StatusChanged and PositionChanged events.
                watcher.StatusChanged += new EventHandler<GeoPositionStatusChang
                edEventArgs>(Watcher_StatusChanged);
                watcher.PositionChanged += new EventHandler<GeoPositionChangedEv
                entArgs<GeoCoordinate>>(Watcher_PositionChanged);

                // Start the location service.
                watcher.Start();
            }
        }
```

Notice that we're attaching two separate event handlers to the GeoCoordinateWatcher instance. The StatusChanged event handler will tell you if the location service is ready and is ready to deliver data to your application. The event handler for the StatusChanged event provides the status of the location service through the GeoPositionStatus enumeration, which has one of the following values: Ready, Disabled, Initializing, or NoData.

The `PositionChanged` event handler is called every time there is a change in the position of the device greater than the threshold defined in the setup of the `GeoCoordinateWatcher` instance. Location data is provided through the `GeoCoordinateWatcher` class. The two event handlers are illustrated here:

```
public void Watcher_StatusChanged(object sender,
    GeoPositionStatusChangedEventArgs e)
{
    string currentStatus = e.Status.ToString();
    statusTextblock.Text = currentStatus;
}


public void Watcher_PositionChanged(object sender, GeoPositionChangedEve
    ntArgs<GeoCoordinate> e)
{
    // Check if location data is available.
    if (e.Position.Location.IsUnknown)
    {
        // Data is not available.
    }
    else
    {
        latitudeTextblock.Text = e.Position.Location.Latitude.ToString();
        longitudeTextblock.Text = e.Position.Location.Longitude.
    ToString();
        altitudeTextblock.Text = e.Position.Location.Altitude.ToString();
        courseTextblock.Text = e.Position.Location.Course.ToString();
        speedTextblock.Text = e.Position.Location.Speed.ToString();
        hAccuracyTextblock.Text = e.Position.Location.HorizontalAccuracy.
    ToString();
        vAccuracyTextblock.Text = e.Position.Location.VerticalAccuracy.
    ToString().ToString();
        timeTextblock.Text = e.Position.Timestamp.ToString();
    }
}
```

You've seen how to obtain the coordinates of the device using location services and display the coordinates in your app. In a real-world application, you'll typically want to display the coordinates in a map. You can use the Bing Maps Silverlight control to display the current position of the device. In order to use the Bing Maps Silverlight control, you need to register for a developer account and obtain a key and a credential token from the Bing Maps portal at www.bingmapsportal.com.

In your application, add a reference to the `Microsoft.Phone.Controls.Map` assembly. Add the `BingMap` control to your XAML as shown here:

```
        <Grid x:Name="ContentPanel" Grid.Row="1" Margin="12,0,12,0">
        <BingMap:Map Name="myBingMap" Margin="10,10,10,60">
            <BingMap:Pushpin Name="bingMapsPushpin"
                Location="47.6395454,-122.130699">
                <BingMap:Pushpin.Content>
                    <Ellipse Fill="Blue" Width="10" Height="10" Name="locator"
                />
                </BingMap:Pushpin.Content>
            </BingMap:Pushpin>
        </BingMap:Map>
    </Grid>
```

In the preceding XAML, we've created a pushpin with its default coordinates (see Figure 13-1). You can design your own pushpin according to the requirement in your application. A pushpin requires its location to be set in XAML or in code.

Figure 13-1: Adding a pushpin on the Bing Maps Silverlight control.

Remember to add the Bing Maps namespace to your XAML, as shown here:

```
xmlns:BingMap="clr-namespace:Microsoft.Phone.Controls.Maps;assembly=Microsoft.
          Phone.Controls.Maps"
```

Once you have set up the pushpin, you can update its position whenever the device receives an update from the location services. In the `Watcher_PositionChanged` event handler, add the following code:

```
Location location = new Location(e.Position.Location.Latitude, e.Position.
          Location.Longitude);bingMapsPushpin.Location = location;
```

You've seen how you can use location service in your app to provide location awareness. Now you can use the Bing Maps service to plot an address using the geocoordinate obtained.

Geofencing

Geofencing is used to notify the user or a trusted party when the device moves in or out of a specified region's boundary. It has applications in location-based services such as tracking trucks on the road for freight forwarding and delivery. It can also be used to tell caregivers when a person leaves a defined area.

Before you commit your life savings to developing an app to find lost children, consult a lawyer. Such apps are very valuable, but they're fraught with legal issues.

A detailed discussion of implementing geofencing is beyond the scope of this book. If you're interested in learning how to implement geofencing in your Windows Phone application, refer to an article by Microsoft employee Dragos Manolescu, available at `http://bit.ly/cWBhpX`.

We highly recommend that you consider the value of geofencing to your app. The use of geofencing within an app is in its early stages, and incorporating it into your app can be one of the ways to make your app stand out. You can find more on this issue in Chapter 17.

Considering Privacy When Working with Location

Location services can drain the battery power from a Windows Phone. Before you set up your app to use location services, you must obtain the permission from the user to access location services. In addition, you must provide the option to turn off location services in your app at a later stage. This feature is mandatory for Marketplace acceptance of your app.

Common services such as Bing search ask for the permission of the user before proceeding to use her location (see Figure 13-2).

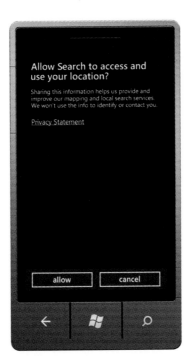

Allow Search to access and use your location?

Sharing this information helps us provide and improve our mapping and local search services. We won't use the info to identify or contact you.

Privacy Statement

allow   cancel

Figure 13-2: Asking for a user's permission before using location services.

Don't let these restrictions keep you from using location information in your app. One of the unique capabilities of cellphones is using the location information. You just need to do so responsibly.

Some privacy advocates have a legitimate concern about the potential for abuse of this information. However, many people don't care that much about their privacy or are willing to risk it for good deals, interesting information about their location, convenience in getting directions, or entertainment. As long as you're offering value in your app and you treat the information according to the guidelines set forth in the Marketplace, you shouldn't hesitate to use this resource.

14

Getting Oriented to the Phone's Orientation

. . . .

In This Chapter

▶ Understanding the importance of the phone's orientation in your application

▶ Updating the layout of your application with orientation changes

. . . .

*I*n Chapter 12, we cover how the accelerometer in Windows Phone 7 can be used to detect the motion of a Windows Phone. We show you how to integrate the readings from the accelerometer within your application. Among the things that the accelerometer can tell your app is the orientation of the phone at any given time.

In this chapter, we explain how to use the orientation of the phone to change between portrait and landscape mode within your application.

Considering the Orientation of the Phone within Your App

You want to provide your users an experience that will make them use your app again and again. And part of how you do that is by ensuring that the user interface (UI) adjusts to the orientation of the device to provide the best viewing angle for the user. For example, when the user is viewing your app while holding the phone in a landscape orientation, your app may display the page with larger fonts. Or you may update the layout by rearranging the controls in the app, making it easier for the user to navigate.

Artville/Getty Images

Windows Phone 7 supports three different orientations: portrait, landscape left, and landscape right. The default orientation of an app is portrait. In portrait orientation, the hardware buttons and the application bar appear toward the bottom of the phone; in landscape left orientation, these items appear to the right of the phone; and in landscape right orientation, they appear to the left of the phone.

If you want, you can restrict your app's orientation to portrait or landscape. You may also let the orientation of the device switch the orientation of the app automatically.

Although you may set your app's orientation to landscape, you won't be able to specify landscape left or landscape right programmatically or in the XAML of any page.

Windows Phone components such as the system tray, volume, ring/vibrate option, push notifications, and dialog boxes change their orientation based on the orientation of the device. The orientation of each control in a page of your app can be set through an attached property of the control. You can use a value converter that converts the current orientation of the page to the correct value of the orientation of the control.

So, whenever the page orientation changes, the orientation of every control in the page will be updated. The complexity in such a scheme is that controls used for layout (such as a Grid) will need their rows and columns swapped to support the updated layout. These controls don't have built-in support for automatically updating their orientation. So, you need to build your own layout control that adapts to changes in the orientation of the phone.

When the user is holding the phone in landscape orientation, the soft input panel (SIP) appears at the bottom when the user is entering text. The SIP can occupy most of the screen's area, so your app needs to adjust to this layout. The design of your app should consider the issue of interface elements hidden beneath the SIP when the user is entering data.

Charles Petzold has written about a technique to deal with orientation changes in a Windows Phone application and presents a Grid control that swaps the rows and columns. You can read this article at `http://bit.ly/980Xsl`.

Using Orientation Information in Your App

In Chapter 12, we show you how the accelerometer in a Windows Phone provides information about its motion and orientation. Although you can use the values from the accelerometer in your application to determine the orientation of the device, you also can use the Windows Phone API to obtain the current orientation of the device.

Using the accelerometer data, you can obtain detailed information about the orientation — for example, whether the phone is in portrait orientation and tilted forward, or in landscape orientation and tilted backward. Such detailed information is required in games and other simulation applications.

When you create a new Windows Phone app in Visual Studio, the XAML of the page has the attribute `SupportedOrientations`. The value of this property determines the orientations supported by your application's page. Its value is set to the enumeration `SupportedPageOrientation`, which has three members: `Portrait`, `Landscape`, and `PortraitOrLandscape`.

The default value of this property set in the XAML is `Portrait`. If you set its value to `Landscape`, the orientation of the page will change to landscape when you view the page in your app running on the phone or in the emulator, as shown in Figure 14-1.

Figure 14-1: Portrait and landscape orientations of a page in an app.

You can obtain the orientation of a page in your app by querying the `Orientation` property of the `PhoneApplicationPage` class. The value of this property is one of the possible values of the `PageOrientation` enumeration (see Figure 14-2):

- **None:** No orientation is specified for the page.
- **Portrait:** The page has portrait orientation.
- **Landscape:** The page has landscape orientation.
- **PortraitUp:** The page has portrait orientation, with the phone controls pointing downward.
- **PortraitDown:** The page has portrait orientation; this orientation is not used.
- **LandscapeLeft:** The page has landscape orientation, with the phone controls to the right.
- **LandscapeRight:** The page has portrait orientation, with the phone controls to the left.

Figure 14-2: Portrait, LandscapeLeft, and LandscapeRight orientations of a page in an app.

The orientation of a page will change whenever the user rotates the device. Windows Phone informs your application of a change in orientation through the OrientationChanged event. You can override the event in your page class as follows:

```
protected override void OnOrientationChanged(OrientationChangedEventArgs e)
{
    // Check the current orientation.
    if (e.Orientation == PageOrientation.Landscape)
    {
        // Update layout of the page
    }
    // Check for Landscape, LandscapeLeft, LandscapeRight.
    else if ((e.Orientation & PageOrientation.Portrait) != 0)
    {
        // Update layout of the page.
    }

    base.OnOrientationChanged(e);
}
```

When the application starts, the phone might be in a landscape mode. The OrientationChanged event is fired, and your application will be able to tap into this event. If the page supports all orientations, the layout of the application can be updated in the overridden method of this event.

You can use animations to update the layout of the application when the user changes the orientation of the device. David Anson has written a detailed article with sample code illustrating how to add animation to changes in orientation. The article is available at http://bit.ly/9obTSr.

After your application receives the OrientationChanged event, you can implement a pattern to handle the change in orientation. The strategy used for adjusting the layout of the application depends on the layout itself. If your application features a media element, such as a picture, buttons to flip to the next or previous picture can be aligned at the bottom of the page below the picture; this will be the default (portrait) layout. When the orientation changes to landscape, the buttons can be moved to the right of the picture, or the buttons can be hidden to allow the picture to occupy the maximum available space.

We'll use a sample application to illustrate how the OrientationChanged event can be used to update its layout when the phone's orientation changes. The snippet of XAML of interest is shown here:

```xml
<!--TitlePanel contains the name of the application and page title-->
<StackPanel x:Name="TitlePanel" Grid.Row="0" Margin="12,17,0,28">
    <TextBlock x:Name="ApplicationTitle" Text="AUTO LAYOUT UPDATE"
        Style="{StaticResource PhoneTextNormalStyle}"/>
    <TextBlock x:Name="PageTitle" Text="Portrait" Margin="9,-7,0,0"
        Style="{StaticResource PhoneTextTitle1Style}"/>
</StackPanel>

<!--ContentPanel - The main layout Grid of the application -->
<Grid x:Name="ContentPanel" Grid.Row="1" Margin="12,0,12,0" >
    <Grid.RowDefinitions>
        <RowDefinition Height="Auto" />
        <RowDefinition Height="*" x:Name="ButtonControlsRow" />
    </Grid.RowDefinitions>
    <Grid.ColumnDefinitions>
        <ColumnDefinition Width="*" />
        <ColumnDefinition x:Name="HiddenColumn" Width="0" />
    </Grid.ColumnDefinitions>
    <TextBlock x:Name="CurrentValue" Text="0.0" FontFamily="Segoe WP"
        FontSize="142"
            Grid.Row="0" Grid.Column="0" HorizontalAlignment="Center"/>
    <!-- ButtonControlsGrid - Grid used for the button controls layout
        -->
    <Grid Grid.Row="1"
        x:Name="ButtonControlsGrid"
        HorizontalAlignment="Center">
      <Grid.RowDefinitions>
          <RowDefinition Height="Auto" />
          <RowDefinition Height="0" />
      </Grid.RowDefinitions>
      <Grid.ColumnDefinitions>
          <ColumnDefinition Width="Auto" />
          <ColumnDefinition Width="Auto" />
      </Grid.ColumnDefinitions>
      <Button x:Name="Increment" Content="Increment" Grid.Row="0"
        Grid.Column="0" />
      <Button x:Name="Decrement" Content="Decrement" Grid.Row="0"
        Grid.Column="1" />
    </Grid>
</Grid>
```

Figure 14-3 shows the application as it appears in Visual Studio.

The application has a `TextBlock` control, the value of which can be increased or decreased with the two buttons. If the app doesn't respond at all to the `OrientationChanged` event, the landscape layout of the application will be as shown in Figure 14-4.

Figure 14-3: A sample Windows Phone application to examine the `OrientationChanged` event.

Figure 14-4: Landscape layout of the application if the `OrientationChanged` event is not used.

Note: You must set the value of the `SupportedOrientations` attribute to `PortraitOrLandscape` in the XAML of the page. The page will then change its orientation to portrait or landscape according to the orientation of the phone.

The layout of the controls as defined in the XAML consists of a Grid (ContentPanel) that has two rows and two columns. In the default portrait orientation, the second column is not visible because its width is set to zero. The second row of this Grid contains another Grid (ButtonControlsGrid) that is used to display the two buttons.

In the OrientationChanged event, if the phone's orientation is landscape, we'll update the app's title, move the ButtonControlsGrid from the second row to the second column of the ContentPanel Grid, and set the height of the second row in the ContentPanel Grid to zero. Therefore, all the controls in the ContentPanel Grid will be in a single row. When the phone's orientation is changed back to portrait, the ButtonControlsGrid will be moved back to the second row of ContentPanel Grid, and the width of the second column in the ContentPanel Grid will be set to zero. In addition, we'll update the position of the two buttons in the ButtonControlsGrid.

Here is the OrientationChanged event that updates the layout of the application:

```
protected override void OnOrientationChanged(OrientationChangedEventArgs e)
    {
        // Check for Landscape, LandscapeLeft, LandscapeRight.
        if ((e.Orientation & PageOrientation.Landscape) != 0)
        {
            // Update layout of the ContentPanel Grid.
            Grid.SetRow(ButtonControlsGrid, 0);
            Grid.SetColumn(ButtonControlsGrid, 1);
            ContentPanel.ColumnDefinitions[1].Width = GridLength.Auto;

            // Update the layout of the ButtonControlsGrid.
            Grid.SetRow(Increment, 0);
            Grid.SetColumn(Increment, 0);
            Grid.SetRow(Decrement, 1);
            Grid.SetColumn(Decrement, 0);
            ButtonControlsGrid.RowDefinitions[1].Height = GridLength.Auto; //
                Set the second row's height
            ButtonControlsGrid.ColumnDefinitions[1].Width = new GridLength(0);
                // Set the second column's width to zero.

            // Change the page title.
            this.PageTitle.Text = "Landscape";
        }
        // Portrait orientation
        else
        {
            // Update layout of the ContentPanel Grid.
            Grid.SetRow(ButtonControlsGrid, 1);
            Grid.SetColumn(ButtonControlsGrid, 0);
            ContentPanel.ColumnDefinitions[1].Width = new GridLength(0);
```

```
    // Update the layout of the ButtonControlsGrid.
    Grid.SetRow(Increment, 0);
    Grid.SetColumn(Increment, 0);
    Grid.SetRow(Decrement, 0);
    Grid.SetColumn(Decrement, 1);
    ButtonControlsGrid.RowDefinitions[1].Height = new GridLength(0); //
        Set the second row's height.
    ButtonControlsGrid.ColumnDefinitions[1].Width = GridLength.Auto; //
        Set the second column's width to zero.

    // Change the page title.
    this.PageTitle.Text = "Portrait";
}

    base.OnOrientationChanged(e);

}
```

Note: The preceding code should be placed inside the `MainPage.xaml.cs` file. It's a new method of the `MainPage` class.

When the phone is held upright with the controls facing down, the default layout is used. In this layout, the `TextBlock` is above the `ButtonControls Grid`. The buttons in the `ButtonControlsGrid` are aligned next to each other. This is show in Figure 14-5.

ContentPanel

ButtonControlsGrid

Figure 14-5: The application in portrait orientation.

In the `OrientationChanged` event, the width of the second column is set to zero, and the buttons are swapped from a single-row, two-column layout to a two-row, single-column layout.

When the orientation of the phone changes to landscape, the buttons are rearranged in the `ButtonControlsGrid`, and it's moved to the second column of the `ContentPanel` Grid. The application in the landscape orientation is shown in Figure 14-6.

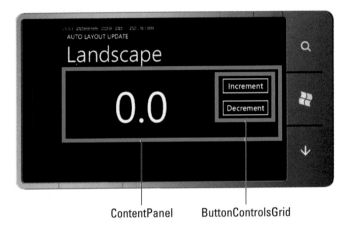

Figure 14-6: The application in landscape orientation.

15

Getting Updates with Push Notification

*M*any mobile apps benefit from being regularly updated with information. For example, an app might show the weather forecast at a particular location. Showing the weather from yesterday when the user first turns on his phone isn't nearly as useful as showing the current readings and latest forecast.

In order for such an app to show the latest information, it needs to periodically query an online service. If an app regularly queries the online service for updated weather data, the app needs to be running all the time or at least as a background process, which can consume battery life and prove to be a nuisance for the user.

The good news is that when Microsoft designed the Windows Phone 7 operating system, it ensured that the battery life of the phone would be maximized, that the phone would always be responsive to the user's input, and that the network usage would be minimal. Multitasking isn't an option in Windows Phone 7, but Microsoft uses push notifications to simulate the behavior of an app that is running in the background.

ImageState

With push notifications, an app doesn't need to be running in order for it to receive updates. When an app has been updated with push notification, data present in the notification is displayed within the app or on the application's tile.

In this chapter, we explore how push notifications work and how you can use them in your apps.

Understanding How Push Notifications Work

The Microsoft Push Notification Service (MPNS) provides developers a platform to incorporate push notifications in their apps. When a web app needs to update the mobile app, the web app sends a push notification to the MPNS. The push notification is then sent to the app on the Windows Phone. After a push notification is sent, the MPNS sends a response code to the web app. The MPNS doesn't provide any confirmation of whether the notification was delivered successfully on the Windows Phone. Figure 15-1 illustrates how push notifications work.

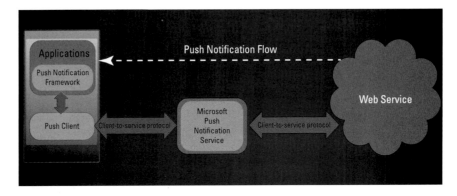

Figure 15-1: How push notifications work.

There are three different types of push notifications:

- **Raw notifications:** Raw notifications are received by an app only when it's running. Raw notifications are useful in conserving the battery power of the phone, but they are not received when the app is closed.

- **Toast notifications:** Toast notifications appear at the top of the phone's screen at all times (see Figure 15-2). Such notifications are visible even when an application is running. A toast notification consists of a title and a message, with an icon of the app. If the user taps the notification, the app is started. This type of notification is displayed only when the app isn't running; it isn't displayed when the app is running. (You're expected to use raw notifications within an app that is running.)

✔ **Tile notifications:** Tile notifications are used to update an app's tile if the tile is pinned to the Start screen of the Windows Phone (see Figure 15-2). Tile notifications are useful when all you need to do is provide a small amount of information (such as an update of the temperature and the forecast or the count of new messages in an instant messaging application) by changing the background image of the tile.

Turning on push notification

Microsoft Marketplace regulations make it mandatory for apps to allow users to turn on and off push notifications. The push notifications settings page should be accessible from within the app at any time (as shown here). Notice that the toggle switch at the top of the page can be used to turn on or off all types of push notifications; if push notifications are turned on, the user can select which notifications to receive.

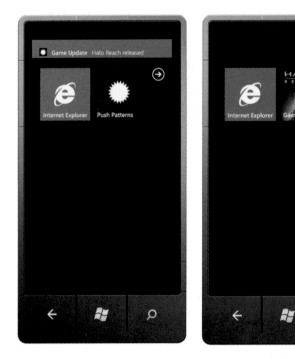

Figure 15-2: Toast notifications (left) and tile notifications (right).

Setting Up Push Notifications within Your App

Throughout this chapter, we use a push notification service sample app made available by Microsoft's Windows Phone team to help developers build Windows Phone apps incorporating push notifications. You can get more details on this sample and download the source code at `http://bit.ly/gqyAP2`; the companion blog article that discusses the sample is available at `http://bit.ly/if3LCn`. **Note:** The source code should be used for learning purposes only.

The sample uses a Windows Presentation Foundation (WPF) app that acts as the server and sends push notifications to the MPNS and a Windows Phone app that registers for the push notifications. The application is shown in Figure 15-3.

If you've downloaded the source code of the push notification service, you can run it to follow the discussion in the rest of this chapter.

Figure 15-3: Push notification sample's server application

Understanding how the Microsoft Push Notification Service works

A Windows Phone application interacts in a certain way with the MPNS and a messaging "server" application. The server application is responsible for sending notifications to the application via the MPNS. The flow of data across the various components is as follows:

1. **A Windows Phone application requests the creation of a new communications channel from the MPNS.**

2. **The MPNS responds to the request from the application with a unique communications channel (a well-formed URL) for the device and the application that requested the channel.**

3. **The newly created communications channel is sent to the server application such that it can send push notifications through the MPNS.**

4. **Whenever the server application needs to send updates to the application, it sends them to the URL of the communications channel.**

5. **A push notification is sent to the Windows Phone by MPNS, and the server application receives an acknowledgement from the MPNS with a response code.**

The communications channel requested by the application is established for the lifetime of the application. In other words, the initial step does not need to be repeated by the application after it's complete. The communications channel is quite robust; it's available even after the phone is turned back on after a loss of power.

Opening the channels of communication

The first step in setting up your Windows Phone application for push notifications is to request a communications channel from the MPNS. You can achieve that as follows:

```
/// <summary>
/// Create channel, subscribe to channel events, and open the channel.
/// </summary>
private void CreateChannel(Action<HttpNotificationChannel> prepared)
{
    // Create a new channel.
    NotificationChannel = new HttpNotificationChannel(ChannelName,
        ServiceName);

    // Register to UriUpdated event. This occurs when channel
    //    successfully opens.
    NotificationChannel.ChannelUriUpdated += (s, e) => Dispatcher.
        BeginInvoke(() => PrepareChannel(prepared));

    SubscribeToNotificationEvents();

    // Trying to open the channel.
    NotificationChannel.Open();
}
```

A new instance of `HttpNotificationChannel` is created with a channel name and service name. The service name is the name used for the server application that will send push notifications to the application. The application then subscribes to the `ChannelUriUpdated` event that is received from the MPNS with the channel's URL. Raw notifications are subscribed to separately by the application.

`HttpNotificationChannel` is the class that encapsulates the communications channel between the application and the MPNS. This class is a part of the `Microsoft.Phone.Notification` namespace.

After the communications channel is received by the application, it registers with the server application that is online to pass the channel URL. Once registered, the server application is able to send push notifications to the Windows Phone app.

Identifying the information in your updates

The server application is used to create the push notification and dispatch it to the Windows Phone app. An application such as a RSS news reader can benefit from push notifications. The server application can download the latest items from an RSS feed and send a push notification with the number of new articles. The user can tap the toast or tile notification, open the application, and read the new items.

The information contained in the notifications differs with the type of notification. When a new push notification arrives, the application can update itself if it's running or inform the user of the update (in the case of toast and tile notifications). The data contained in a raw notification is extracted from the HttpNotificationEventArgs argument, as follows:

```
/// <summary>
    /// Parse the raw notification received.
    /// </summary>
    /// <param name="sender"></param>
    /// <param name="e"></param>
    private void httpRawNotificationReceived(object sender,
            HttpNotificationEventArgs e)
    {
        if (e.Notification.Body != null) // Notification contains valid data.
        {
            System.IO.StreamReader reader = new System.IO.StreamReader(e.
            Notification.Body);
            Dispatcher.BeginInvoke(() => { txtMessage.Text = "Raw Notification
            Message Received: " + reader.ReadToEnd(); });
        }
    }
```

Toast notifications received when the application is running can be intercepted by the application if the ShellToastNotificationReceived event is handled. When the application is not running, the toast notification appears as a pop-up; tapping the pop-up opens the application. You can implement an event handler for the ShellToastNotificationReceived event as follows:

```
/// <summary>
    /// Parse the toast notification received.
    /// </summary>
    /// <param name="sender"></param>
    /// <param name="e"></param>
```

(continued)

(continued)

```
private void shellToastNotificationReceived(object sender,
    NotificationEventArgs e)
{
    if (e.Collection != null) // Notification contains valid data.
    {
        Dictionary<string, string> collection = (Dictionary<string,
            string>)e.Collection;
        System.Text.StringBuilder messageBuilder = new System.Text.
            StringBuilder();
        foreach (string elementName in collection.Keys)
        {
            txtMessage.Text += string.Format("Key: {0}, Value:{1}\r\n",
            elementName, collection[elementName]);
        }
    }
}
```

Tile notifications cannot be intercepted by an application on the phone. These notifications update the application's tile if it's pinned by the user to the Start screen on the phone.

Dispatching the notification

The push notification framework allows the server application to send an array of bytes as a raw notification. Unlike toast and tile notifications, raw notifications allow the server to send data as an array of bytes (for example, a string, an image, and so on). Here's the code used to send a raw notification:

```
private void SendRawNotification(string message)
{
    HttpWebRequest rawNotificationRequest = (HttpWebRequest)WebRequest.
        Create(message);
    rawNotificationRequest.Method = "POST";
    rawNotificationRequest.Headers = new WebHeaderCollection();
    rawNotificationRequest.ContentType = "text/xml";
    rawNotificationRequest.Headers.Add("X-WindowsPhone-Target", "");
    rawNotificationRequest.Headers.Add("X-NotificationClass", "3"); //
        Raw notification
    byte[] strBytes = new UTF8Encoding().GetBytes(message);
    rawNotificationRequest.ContentLength = strBytes.Length;

    // Start sending the request and parse the response status.
    using (Stream requestStream = rawNotificationRequest.
        GetRequestStream())
    {
        requestStream.Write(strBytes, 0, strBytes.Length);
    }
    HttpWebResponse response = (HttpWebResponse)rawNotificationRequest.
        GetResponse();
    string rawNotificationStatus = response.Headers["X-
        NotificationStatus"];
```

```
        string deviceConnectionStatus = response.Headers["X-
            DeviceConnectionStatus"];
    }
```

Note that the notification type is added in the header of the
`HttpWebRequest` object.

In order for a tile notification to be sent to the application, you need to
modify a few lines of the code shown above. The stream of bytes needs to be
prepared with an XML template that identifies the background image URL,
the count, and the title displayed on the tile. Here is the XML required to
send a toast notification:

```
        <?xml version=\"1.0\" encoding="utf-8"?>
        <wp:Notification xmlns:wp="WPNotification">
        <wp:Tile>
        <wp:BackgroundImage>URI for Background Image</wp:BackgroundImage>
        <wp:Count>Count</wp:Count>
        <wp:Title>Title</wp:Title>
        </wp:Tile>
        </wp:Notification>
```

Note that the fields highlighted in bold in the XML shown above need to be
updated for the notification. The `BackgroundImage` XML element specifies
the location on the internet of the tile's background image. The `Count` and
`Title` XML elements are used to specify the count and title values placed
on the application's tile. After this XML is formatted, it is converted into a
stream of bytes and sent as a push notification. Note that the following two
lines of code need to be updated for sending the notification:

```
    tileNotificationRequest.Headers.Add("X-WindowsPhone-Target", "token");
        tileNotificationRequest.Headers.Add("X-NotificationClass", "1"); //
            Tile notification
```

Toast notifications require the message to be prepared as XML, similar to tile
notifications. Here's the XML used for sending toast notifications:

```
        <?xml version="1.0" encoding="utf-8"?>
        <wp:Notification xmlns:wp="WPNotification">
        <wp:Toast>
        <wp:Text1>Title</wp:Text1>
        <wp:Text2>Content</wp:Text2>
        </wp:Toast>
        </wp:Notification>
```

Note that the fields highlighted in the XML needs to be updated for the notification. The title field in the XML specifies the title of the notification, and the
content field specifies the body of the message. The following lines of code
need to be updated for sending the notification:

```
toastNotificationRequest.Headers.Add("X-WindowsPhone-Target", "toast");
        toastNotificationRequest.Headers.Add("X-NotificationClass", "2"); //
            Toast notification
```

Managing your updates

The push notification framework provides a unique way of updating a Windows Phone app without the intervention of the user. When you're developing apps with push notifications, note that there is a limit of only one communications channel per app and there can be a maximum of 15 push notification channels per Windows Phone device. If either of these limits is exceeded, an exception will be thrown within the app, and it won't receive push notifications.

Windows Marketplace requirements specify that you should allow the user to opt out of push notifications. Your app needs to ask the user's permission to receive push notifications when the application is first run. The push notification settings page should be easily accessible from within the application.

Finally, to ensure privacy, data sent in push notifications should not be used to identify the user.

Updating the application tile

There is an alternative to using push notifications to update your application's tile. The alternative uses the `ShellTileSchedule` class in the `Microsoft.Phone.Shell` namespace. The following code sample shows how you can implement tile updates in your app:

```
private void ApplicationTileUpdate()
{
    ShellTileSchedule tileSchedule = new
        ShellTileSchedule();
    tileSchedule.RemoteImageUri = new Uri("http://
        yoururl.com/firstimage.png");
    tileSchedule.Interval = UpdateInterval.EveryHour;
    tileSchedule.Recurrence = UpdateRecurrence.Interval;
    tileSchedule.StartTime = DateTime.Now;
    tileSchedule.MaxUpdateCount= 0; // Run indefinitely
    tileSchedule.Start();
}
```

Note that if `MaxUpdateCount` is not set or is set to a number less than 1, the updates will continue to occur indefinitely while your app is actively running on the phone. The minimum interval at which an update is run is an hour.

Part V
Leveraging the Windows Phone Marketplace

The 5th Wave   By Rich Tennant

Of course it doesn't make any sense, but it's our only chance! Now hook the Windows Phone into the override and see if you can bring this baby in.

In this part . . .

The only source for apps on a Windows Phone is the Marketplace. You need to get your app out in the Marketplace for anyone to use it.

The chapters in this part cover the process for getting your app listed in the Marketplace. More important, this part covers the tools and methods you need to stand out in the crowd of available apps.

Photo credits: Digital Vision (top, middle, bottom)

16

Working the Microsoft Approval Process

In This Chapter

▶ Following Microsoft's rules

▶ Preparing to submit your app

▶ Avoiding the pitfalls

▶ Setting realistic expectations

▶ Knowing what to do if your app is rejected

*T*his is the moment you've been waiting for: your chance to submit your app to the Marketplace! Submitting your app can be difficult, so the purpose of this chapter is to make it as simple and straightforward as possible. We do this by reviewing the rules, helping you get set up for the process, and demystifying what goes on behind the screen.

When it comes to designing apps for mobile devices, Microsoft is middle of the road. Apple has a reputation for being particularly stringent; Android tends to allow apps through quickly, with relatively little screening; and Microsoft falls somewhere in between. ***Remember:*** The goal is to ensure that apps won't cause problems for the phone or the user.

Corbis Digital Stock

Reviewing the Rules of the Road

Before you dive into the submittal process, take a minute to review Microsoft's rules. You'd hate to spend a lot of time submitting your app only to have it rejected because you forgot to dot your *i*'s and cross your *t*'s.

✔ Your app can't crash or hang when running hard or when sitting idle for a long time.

✔ Your app can't have any generic or vague error messages.

✔ The first screen of your app must show up within 5 seconds of launch. In that first 5 seconds, you can provide a splash screen image in a file called `SplashScreenImage.jpg`. You still need to be up and running in under 5 seconds, though.

✔ Your app must be able to take user input within 20 seconds.

✔ Your app can't interfere with a phone call, SMS message, or MMS message. You app can't be affected by an incoming phone call, SMS message, or MMS message.

✔ You must be internally consistent with respect to language. For example, if you write for the Italian language, the splash screen, the descriptions, the screenshots, and the error messages must all be in Italian. In other words, you can't be lazy on your translation.

✔ Your app must be able to accept the user's choice to turn off the GPS information, either by working around it or by telling the user that turning off the GPS makes the app not work. You also have to tell users that you're using their GPS info in your app (if you are).

✔ Some users have a timer that locks their screen if unused for a period of time. Your app should be okay with that.

✔ You can't do anything that gets you out of the sandbox. The application must release exclusive resources when moved into the background.

✔ Your app can play music or videos and work with photos. Your app can't disable or otherwise mess up the existing Microsoft apps that come standard with the phone.

✔ Your app can't include abusive, "unnecessary" foul language, or encouragement to do anything mean, nasty, or rotten to anyone, particularly protected groups or groups that should be protected. (This is a subjective rule, but Microsoft is interested in avoiding controversy with users by being restrictive with developers.)

✔ Violence in games is common, but it can't be over the top. You can have a shooter game, but splattering blood or brains is out. This issue is subjective, of course, and Microsoft tries to negotiate without being too restrictive.

✔ Your app should be G or PG. The best guide is to imagine showing your app to a child younger than 13 years old with his or her parents present. If you're not sure whether something is appropriate, leave it out. Windows Phone 7 is not intended to be part of the sexual revolution. If your intent is to tap into the huge pornography market, you've picked the wrong platform.

✔ You can't use the intellectual property of others without permission. This may seem obvious, but plagiarism is a crime. Be sure you have written consent from the person or company that owns the item(s) in question. Branded content can be used only with permission.

✔ It is frowned upon for your app to steal information, scam money from the user, or ruin the phone. Microsoft will check your app to be sure your app doesn't do these things intentionally and will look for any viruses that may have tried to sneak in on your app.

The Microsoft legalese for these rules is in the document Windows Phone 7 Application Certification Requirements, found in the Microsoft Developers Portal at `http://create.msdn.com` (see Chapter 6).

Fasten Your Seat Belt: Getting Ready to Submit Your App

When you're satisfied with your app, your work is not yet done. You need to have about a dozen items ready before you can begin the submission process:

✔ The iconography for the user to buy your app from the Marketplace or to launch your app from his phone

✔ Your application description, which includes the following:

- The formal title of your app

- A description of your app

- Screenshots from your app

- Customer service contact information

✔ Plans for categorization within the Marketplace, which include the following:

- Which languages you support

- Which countries you want to market your app in

- Which app categories you want to be in

✔ Your Windows Live ID

✔ Information Microsoft needs so you can be paid

✔ Your bundled app created by Visual Studio (see the end of Chapter 8 for more on bundling your app)

For more on each of these subjects, read on.

Icons

When you submit your app, you need five icons:

- ✔ **Small app icon:** The small app icon is 62 x 62 pixels. It's used for the app list on the phone to launch your application.

- ✔ **Small mobile app tile:** The small mobile app tile is 99 x 99 pixels. This tile is used on a phone when someone is scrolling through the Marketplace.

- ✔ **Large mobile app tile:** The large mobile app tile is 173 x 173 pixels. This tile is also used on a phone when someone is scrolling through the Marketplace.

- ✔ **Large PC app tile:** The large PC app tile is 200 x 200 pixels. This tile is used within the PC version of the Marketplace.

- ✔ **Background art:** Background art is 1,000 by 800 pixels. It's really a hybrid between a screen background and an icon and captures the color theme used in your app. You need background art if you want to be selected as a featured app (which, trust us, you want).

All these icons should be in PNG format. Figure 16-1 shows the relative sizes of the first four icons and tiles, using the WeatherBug application as an example.

Microsoft sometimes refer to these as icons and other times as tiles. Don't worry so much about the name — just focus on making sure you have the PNG files listed earlier.

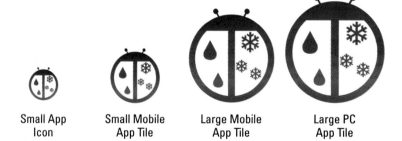

| Small App | Small Mobile | Large Mobile | Large PC |
| Icon | App Tile | App Tile | App Tile |

Figure 16-1: The icon files for the WeatherBug app.

The four images do not need to be identical. The icons should be similar in style, but you can get somewhat fancier with the larger tiles.

Just because you have the skills to be a good programmer doesn't mean you have the skills to make exciting icons. It takes some time to find an icon that effectively captures the essence of your app and stands out in the crowd. If you plan ahead, you can find a good graphic artist who can help you capture the essence of your app. If hiring someone is too complicated or costly, many web-based companies will license you an icon from their inventory — try Glossy Icon (www.glossyicon.com), IconEasy (www.iconeasy.com), or Icon Empire (www.iconempire.com).

We can't overstate the importance of a good icon. A weak icon will cause potential customers to overlook your great work.

The application description

The application description is another aspect of the submission process that you need to have prepared before you submit your app. You may think that you should be able prepare the app description while you're waiting for the app to be tested — after all, it would be a good use of the downtime. No such luck. You need to be prepared at the time of app submission with the application description. The main reason: Part of the submission involves making sure that the app you submit is consistent with what you describe.

Figure 16-2 shows a representative application description.

Here are the major elements that you should prepare:

- ✔ **The application title:** This may seem obvious, but you need to put a stake in the ground and name your app. Up to this point, you may have been using a working title. It's time to make your choice.

  Ideally, the product name captures the essence of the app, tells what is unique about the app, and is clever.

- ✔ **The description and a bulleted list of features:** You get about 50 words to capture the imagination of your audience and tell them what your app is and what makes it different from the other apps in the category. You then have about five bullet points to complement your description. The challenge is to make each word count.

- ✔ **Application requirements:** Largely an artifact from the earlier days when Windows Mobile had many different hardware variations, this covers any capabilities that are necessary on the phone in order to run your app. For the initial release of Windows Phone 7, there are no relevant differences among different brands as far as your app is concerned. Therefore, you could just put, "Must use Windows Phone 7 hardware."

- ✔ **The release date:** The app cannot be released until it passes submittal, but you can't submit without putting in a release date. Just use the date of submission as the release date.

- ✔ **The version number:** Your first version will be version 1.0. Using the conventional numbering scheme, you increment enhancements and bug fixes in the tenths column. Your first enhancement would be version 1.1; your second enhancement, version 1.2; and so on. You switch to version 2.0 when you have a number of new features. (Turn to Chapter 20 for more on version numbers and app updates.)

✔ **The size of the file:** This is the physical size of the XAP file you're submitting. The Windows Phone can easily store your app, regardless of its size, unless you've gone completely overboard. Nevertheless, you need to tell the user the size of your app. For reference, your app and all the supporting information have to be less than 225 MB. In practice, your app will probably be measured in KB rather than in MB.

✔ **Company contact information:** You need to provide marketing information and customer support (see Chapter 21).

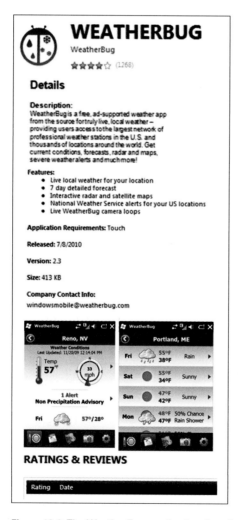

Figure 16-2: The WeatherBug application description.

Marketplace categorization

In order to properly categorize your app, you have to make a series of decisions. The three choices you have for categorization are the following:

- **Which languages you support:** The Windows Phone currently supports five languages (six if you count International English):

  - English

  - English (International)

  - French

  - German

  - Italian

  - Spanish

  Chances are, you picked a language before you started writing your app.

  Keep in mind that it isn't heroic to have your app translated into other languages — it just opens new markets without the difficulty associated with writing an entirely new app from scratch. (See Chapter 18 for more on selling your app to the international market.)

- **Countries in which you want to market your app:** A simple answer would be to market your app in every country that speaks the language used by your app, but it isn't quite that easy. There are a few other considerations:

  - Windows Phone 7 is not available in every country.

  - Your app may use words or colloquialisms that are confusing or if not properly localized.

  - Your app may be rated G or PG by local standards, but other cultures may have sensitivities that may surprise you.

  - Some images or even shared code may be open source in some countries, but not all.

  As of this writing, Windows Phone 7 is available in 30 countries. The folks in Redmond are doing what they can to increase this count. It's a waste of time to customize an app for a country that doesn't yet have Windows Phone 7.

- **Which app category you want to be in:** In Chapter 4, we present the app categories along with descriptions.

Your Windows Live ID

You need your Windows Live ID to submit your app. If you don't yet have your Windows Live ID, turn to Chapter 5 for more information.

Payment information

You need to provide some financial information so that you can get paid when your app sells. In this section, we fill you in on what you need to provide.

Deciding on the legal entity

A clearly identified legal entity must engage in the submission of your app. That sounds a lot more complicated than it really is. You can submit your app as an individual, or you can submit it as a company.

If you haven't already created a company that has a taxpayer ID number, the decision is clear: You as an individual will submit the app. Even though you may have written the app with a partner, getting incorporated and obtaining a tax ID number will take you a long time. We hope that you can trust each other, at least for the first submission. You can see about changing the legal entity, if necessary, for version 1.1.

If you're submitting as an individual, you'll need to supply your Social Security number. The income will be assigned to you personally, and you'll be liable for the taxes. If you have a corporation and want the money to go to your company, you'll need to have your taxpayer ID number.

Paying to play

You'll need to pay a fee of $99 to become a registered user. Yes, it would be nice if it were free, but look at it this way: This nominal fee keeps out the riffraff — it sets a minimum standard that the folks who are putting out applications have at least something on the ball and won't clutter the Windows Marketplace with useless apps that frustrate your customers.

Getting paid

In order to be paid, you'll need to provide the bank account where you want the fruits of your labor to be deposited.

Getting validated

Forget the idea of making up a Social Security number or taxpayer ID number. An identity validation process assists Microsoft in weeding out any individuals or groups that have bad intentions.

The validation is performed by a third party called GeoTrust, which specializes in making sure that you really are you. (If you have any self-doubt, this process should make you feel better about yourself!) Getting validated usually takes a couple days. The good news is that the application can be submitted and begin its journey before the GeoTrust process is complete.

If you're a registered developer with an active account, you've already gone through this process.

You have to submit your bank's routing numbers and your account number. You can find this information on one of your checks (see Figure 16-3) or contact your bank for the information.

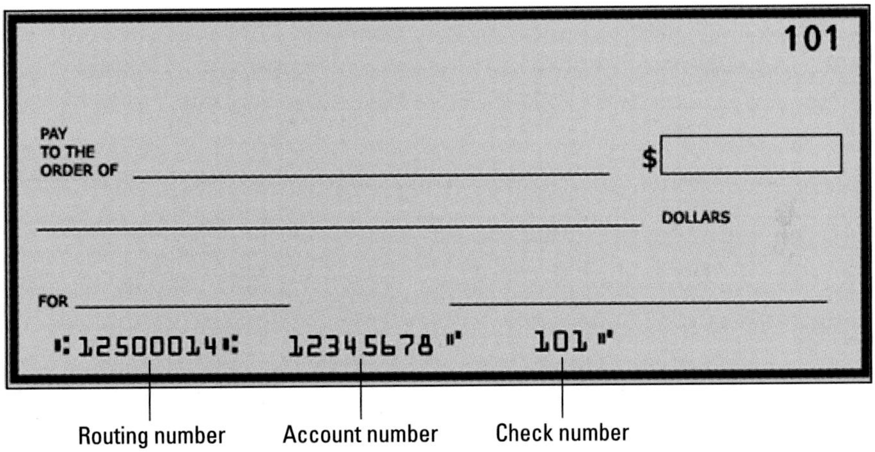

Figure 16-3: Where to find the routing and account numbers on a check.

XAP file packaging

The last step is to bundle all the files together in one bigger XAP file. You do this within Visual Studio. The files you need to bundle are

✔ The file manifest, which describes the contents

✔ The assembly files, which include the logic of your application

✔ The images that make up the app, including the background, the splash screens, and the warning screens

You create the XAP file from within Visual Studio. If you've debugged your app, the XAP file is sitting there, waiting for you to open it and send it on its way. (If you haven't debugged your app with the Windows Phone Emulator, refer to Chapter 5.)

To find the XAP file, look in the `Bin/Debug` folder. If you're having trouble finding it, follow these steps from within Visual Studio:

1. **Click the Open icon to open the files associated with your project.**

   The Open File dialog box (shown in Figure 16-4) appears.

2. **Click the `Bin` folder.**

3. **Click the `Debug` folder.**

   And there it is! The XAP file is sitting there, all ready for your submission!

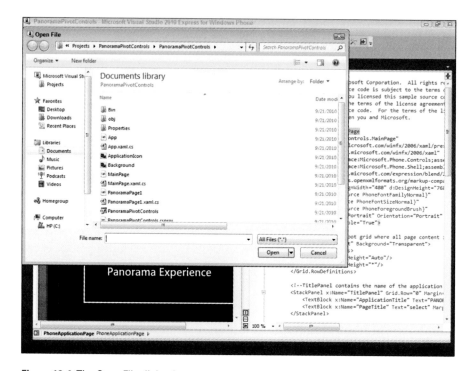

Figure 16-4: The Open File dialog box.

Stepping Through the Processes

You've assembled all the information and files you need to start the submission process. The next two steps — registration and submission — will flow smoothly.

We present these steps together, but you can actually register long before you're ready to submit your app.

Registration

Before you get started in the registration process, go to `https://users.create.msdn.com/Register` and sign in with your Windows Live ID. When you're signed in, you'll see the screen shown in Figure 16-5.

The website implies that there are only five steps in this process. The actual number of steps depends on whether you're an Xbox Live user who has already established an account and stored a credit card on your account. We take the complete route to cover our bases.

Now, follow these steps:

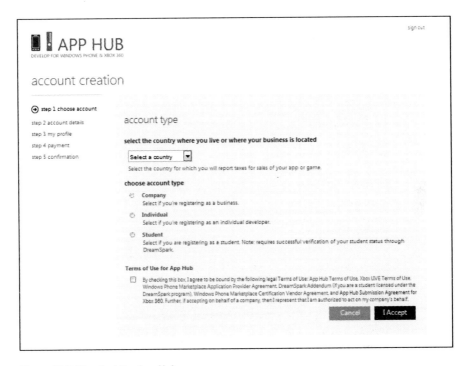

Figure 16-5: Step 1 of the App Hub.

1. **Select your country from the drop-down list and choose your account type; read the Terms of Use and accept them.**

   The screen shown in Figure 16-6 appears if you're signing up for an individual account.

2. **Enter your personal information, and click Next.**

   The screen shown in Figure 16-7 appears.

3. **Choose a profile image, and click Next.**

   The profile image is used when you get involved in the community of developers who share tips, techniques, and advice. To make this experience more personal, each participant in the community needs a profile image.

   After you've chosen a profile image, the screen shown in Figure 16-8 appears.

4. **Read the Terms of Use, and click Accept.**

   Don't ask why you have to accept a Terms of Use on the first registration page and again here.

   After you've accepted the Terms of Use, the page shown in Figure 16-9 appears.

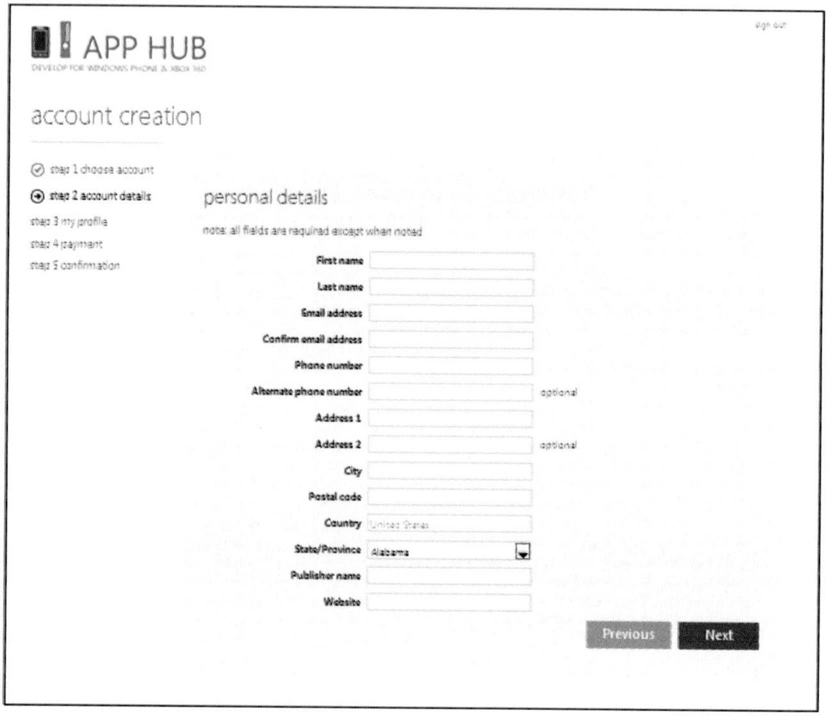

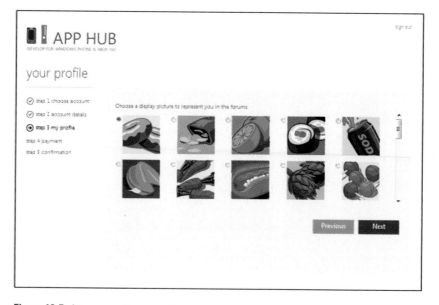

Figure 16-6: Let the registration begin!

Figure 16-7: Are you sushi or soda?

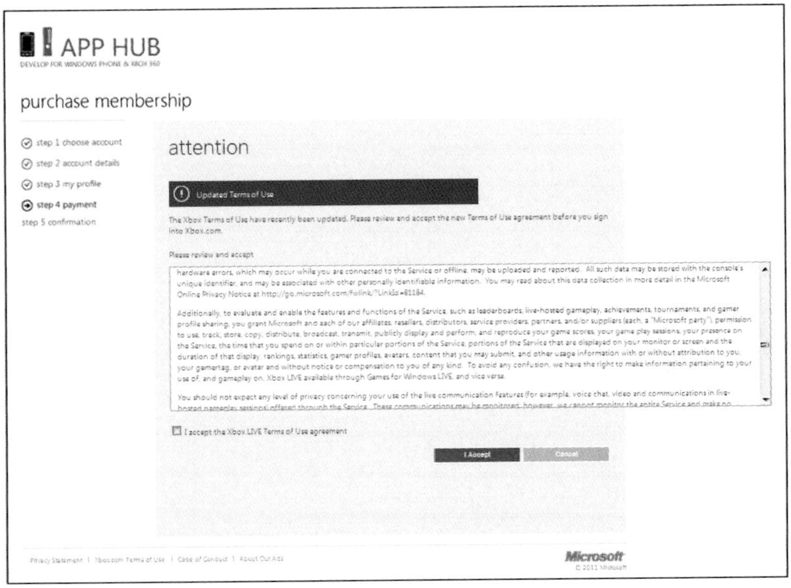

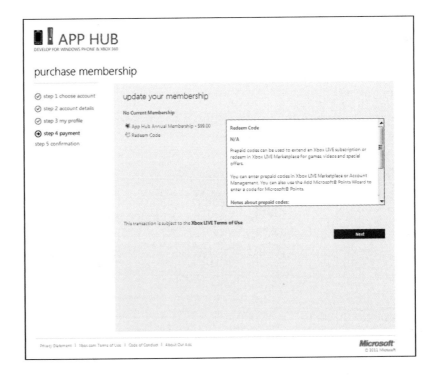

Figure 16-8: More Terms of Use.

Figure 16-9: Select a membership.

5. Click the App Hub Annual Membership button, and click Next.

This brings you to the screen shown in Figure 16-10.

Figure 16-10: Pay for your membership.

6. Select a credit card to pay for your membership, and click Next.

If you haven't stored a credit card with Microsoft before, click the Add a New Credit Card link; you'll be taken to the screen shown in Figure 16-11. Enter your payment information, and click Save. You're back at the screen shown in Figure 16-10. Now select your card, and click Next.

After you've selected your card, you see the screen shown in Figure 16-12. The verification process begins.

After you're verified, you have access to your Dashboard (see Figure 16-13). The Dashboard welcomes you with the message, "Hey! You don't have any apps yet." Say, "No duh," and move on.

![APP HUB screen showing purchase membership form]

APP HUB
DEVELOP FOR WINDOWS PHONE & XBOX 360

purchase membership

- ✓ step 1 choose account
- ✓ step 2 account details
- ✓ step 3 my profile
- ● step 4 payment
- step 5 confirmation

complete your purchase

Please enter all information exactly as it appears on your credit card.

Your credit card will not be charged at this time.
This transaction is subject to the **Xbox LIVE Terms of Use**

Credit Card Type

> Visa

Credit Card Number

Expiration Date

> 04   2011

Security code

> What is this?

Card Holder Name

> Santa Claus

Address Line 1

> One Icicle Lane

Address Line 2 (optional)

City

> North Pole

State

> ALASKA

Postal Code

> 98121

Country/Region

United States

| Back | Save | Cancel |

Privacy Statement   Xbox.com Terms of Use   Code of Conduct   About Our Ads

Microsoft
©2011 Microsoft

Figure 16-11: Enter your credit card information.

App submission

While the background verification is under way, you can submit your app. Of course, if any problems come up in the registration process, your app won't make it to the Marketplace.

During the submission process, you can save and close at any time if you need more time to think about an answer. You'll just pick up later where you left off.

Figure 16-12: You're all done registering.

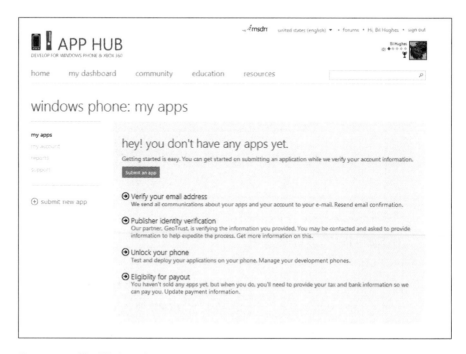

Figure 16-13: The Windows Phone App Hub Dashboard.

To start the submission process, follow these steps:

1. **Click the blue square that says Submit an App (refer to Figure 16-13).**

   The page shown in Figure 16-14 appears.

Figure 16-14: The Upload screen.

2. **Complete this page, upload your app, and click Next.**

   The page shown in Figure 16-15 appears.

3. **Enter the application description, and click Next.**

   The page shown in Figure 16-16 appears.

windows phone: submit new app

step 1 upload
step 2 description
step 3 artwork
step 4 pricing
step 5 submit

⊕ back to dashboard

description | English (International)

Application title Margie's Travel Game

Supported languages English (International)
You are currently editing this application in English (International).

Category ⓘ Games ▼   Sub-category Puzzle & Trivia ▼

Detailed description

Featured app description Travel Game ⓘ
(optional)

Keywords Margie, travel, game ⓘ

ESRB rating & certificate None ▼   Browse ⓘ
(optional)

PEGI rating & certificate None ▼   Browse ⓘ
(optional)

USK rating & certificate None ▼   Browse ⓘ
(optional)

Legal URL (optional)

Support email address support@margiestravel.com
(optional)

Required device capabilities Package validation in progress. Capabilities will appear here once validation completes.

Push notification certificates None ▼ ⓘ
(optional)

All fields on this page are required unless noted. You may continue to the next screen once the required fields have been populated.

Previous   Next   Save & Quit

Figure 16-15: The Description screen.

4. Select the radio buttons, upload the images, and click Next.

The page shown in Figure 16-17 appears.

5. Enter the price, and click Next.

The page shown in Figure 16-18 appears.

Normally, you would want to launch your app as soon as possible after it has been tested and verified. However, you have the option, by unchecking the box, to have your app hit the Marketplace at a later date that you control.

windows phone: submit new app

upload app artwork | English (International)

step 1 upload
step 2 description
step 3 artwork
step 4 pricing
step 5 submit

⊕ back to dashboard

Large mobile app tile
File type: PNG
173 x 173px 96 DPI

Small mobile app tile
File type: PNG
99 x 99px 96DPI

Large PC app tile
File type: PNG
200 x 200px 96 DPI

Background art
File type: PNG
1000 x 800px 96DPI
Optional

Screenshots
Click to add up to 8 images
File type: PNG
480 x 800px 96DPI
Optional   Optional

Optional   Optional   Optional

Optional   Optional

All fields on this page are required unless noted. You may continue to the next screen once the required fields have been populated.

Previous   Next   Save & Quit

Figure 16-16: The Upload App Artwork screen.

The approval process may take a while. First, the app must be analyzed for what will appear in the catalog; this includes the title, the description, and the icons. Then the app is packaged — the app is licensed and examined from a compliance standpoint. This is followed by certification and finally code signing. The process is somewhat automated, but there is a human component.

After your app passes certification, a VeriSign certificate is issued. You'll be informed, and your app will be placed in the Marketplace.

If your app is denied, you'll need to fix all reported issues before you can resubmit your app for certification.

Figure 16-17: The Price Your App screen.

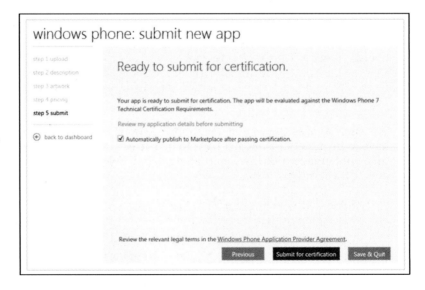

Figure 16-18: The Ready to Submit for Certification screen.

Standing Out from the Crowd

*T*he brutal reality is that the brilliance of your programming or the value inherent in your idea is lost unless your audience downloads your app. Users have thousands of apps to consider. Your job is to offer them sufficient information in the right situations to get them to try your app.

There are two primary ways in which you want to get noticed: within the Marketplace and through external marketing. We cover both in this chapter.

Getting Noticed in the Marketplace

According to an old parable, two hunters were caught in the woods without their guns when an angry bear began charging. The first hunter started running. The second hunter yelled, "Hey! You can't outrun a bear!" The first hunter yelled back, "I don't have to outrun the bear — I just have to outrun you!"

Corbis Digital Stock

The same applies to you and your app: You don't have to be perfect — you just have to be better than your competition. And you can do that by following these suggestions:

▸ **Make your icon eye-catching.** Bright colors and sharp graphics help (see Chapter 16).

▸ **Make it obvious what your content is.** Confused customers don't buy. They just go on to find less confusing options.

▸ **Choose a good name.** The right name grabs the user's attention and conveys the purpose of the app. *Remember:* There are thousands of apps out there — you have only a few seconds to grab a potential user's attention, and the name is an important part of doing that.

You can't determine how attractive you are without watching your competition. You can't just check the Marketplace for your competition before you submit your app and leave it at that. You need to continually monitor your competition and tune your message to address your customers just a bit better than your competition does.

Don't expect your competitors to throw in the towel. When you're successful, they'll fight back by offering a new release with updated marketing. And they'll claim that their new release is "new and improved."

App development is an iterative process. It never ends. Don't let yourself be complacent with your success — if you do, a hungrier competitor will steal your position. You may as well be the one to up the ante with new releases and updated logos and descriptions faster than your competition to keep them off balance.

Ideally, you should update your marketing message every six to eight months, depending upon the number of competitors you have and the complexity of the application category.

In the following sections, we cover some more ways you can make sure your app stands out from the crowd.

Writing a compelling description

After the icon and the name, the description is your best chance of selling your product. You have only a few sentences to capture your customer's attention. You need to be brief but descriptive.

Use simple declarative sentences. Set yourself apart from the rest of the crowd. Think about what's unique to your app and capitalize on this difference. (Can't think of anything? You may want to go back to the drawing board.)

Categorizing your app

You can choose only one category for your app. If you're really torn between two categories, or even among multiple categories, you can offer several versions of your app. Do this judiciously, however, and make sure that there are some differences among the various versions. Renaming the app for different categories and changing nothing else about the app would be a mistake — users will find out about this and let others know. This may lead to negative comments accusing you of being lazy, rather than being creative in making your app more available.

Yet another option is to have several versions available with different images within the app. Let's say you make a solitaire app, an app that appeals to people from all walks of life, but you make it more attractive to enthusiasts of the sport of curling by including images of stones and curling brooms on your deck of cards. Now, let's say you make another version of the app that includes images of caber tossing on your deck of cards — you'll draw in enthusiasts of that sport and broaden your segment of the marketplace.

Offering a trial version

Offering a trial version and a full-featured version is a tried-and-true method of getting prospective customers to consider your app. If your competition doesn't offer a free trial version (or one for a very low price), and you do, users will be more likely to go with you than your competition.

It works the other way, too: If you don't offer a trial and your competition does, you may have the best app in the world, but your customers will never know because trying your competition is less risky for them.

The trial app you offer can have limited features, or it may allow only a specific number of uses before the user has to upgrade to the full-featured app. The main objective is to get prospective customers hooked so that shifting to another app feels like a foreign experience.

Becoming a featured application

One of the best ways to stand out from the crowd is to become a featured application. If your app is selected, it's featured on the panorama and seen by everyone who opens the Marketplace hub on the phone (see Figure 17-1). This means that your app will be the first one that someone sees in your category. It doesn't cost money to be selected as the featured app. The challenge is to be picked by the folks within the Marketplace for this position.

The only hitch is that Microsoft hasn't published its recipe for selecting featured apps. Looking at the kinds of applications that have been featured in the past, we can infer that they offer some unique capability or different approach to stand out from the crowd.

Focus your creativity on being better than your competition, and even if you don't end up a featured app, you'll be ahead of the game.

You can't pay Microsoft for placement within the Marketplace. You won't be notified if your app is featured. Suddenly, one day it'll be there. In fact, you may find out by checking your Dashboard and finding a large check waiting for you!

Getting good ratings

Good ratings come from making a realistic promise and then meeting or exceeding it.

Figure 17-1: Being featured on the Marketplace hub is a great form of free advertising!

In a perfect world, you would've been able to thoroughly test your app with users before your launch. That's the traditional way that manufacturers test their products. But that isn't possible with the restriction of no side-loading of apps on the Windows Phone.

Instead, you have to launch the app in the Marketplace, and while you're getting your first customers, test your app with them. If or when you find problems that didn't show up on the Windows Phone Emulator, fix them quickly and release a new revision. Plan this extra app iteration into your schedule.

Most users are fairly forgiving if the app performs well and unforgiving if the app isn't stable or doesn't deliver as promised. Having a groundbreaking and astounding app is less important than having an app that does what it says it will.

Sure, bad reviews hurt your feelings, but more important, they scare away many prospective customers.

Leveraging Other Marketing Tools

Leverage the tools on the Marketplace as best you can. The Marketplace is the only place where users can go to get apps. When they're there, they're in a buying mode. But nothing limits you from marketing your Windows Phone app in other locations. In fact, Microsoft would love to see you market your app in other venues. They won't help you with resources to market your app, but it may make you feel better that someone in Redmond will smile at your efforts to market your Windows Phone app through other media.

Promoting through targeted media

If you followed our earlier recommendations, you designed your app with a particular market segment (also known as a *niche*) in mind. For example, if you're making a poker game, having the players wear shirts from different schools may catch the eye of loyal alumnae. Chances are, an alumni magazine serves that alumni group. Promoting in that magazine is usually pretty cheap.

You need to get a license, or at least permission, to use the logo of any organization. If, by some chance, the unauthorized use of a logo gets by Microsoft in the submission process, you would eventually get a cease-and-desist letter at a minimum. Dot your *i*'s and cross your *t*'s, and get permission!

Taking this approach further, you can find magazines and mailing lists that serve a loyal audience, and customize your app specifically for them. This allows you to take a generic app that may be of interest to some people and make it really unique and of interest to a specific group.

The challenge is that you have to manage several apps at once. Instead of seeing this as a problem, think of it as an opportunity. For example, does Campbell's really need a hundred varieties of soup when three or four varieties are the most popular? Having that large number of varieties gives Campbell's more shelf space at the supermarket and gets the consumer to think more about his options before making a choice. Instead of trying to be efficient and limit the offerings to just the top three, Campbell's allows each consumer to feel better about his choice. Plus, Campbell's likely broadens its overall customer reach because some people never buy those top-three soups and prefer other varieties instead.

Sure, it would be easier to manage and update one app. But if you offer variations of apps that resonate with loyal groups, you may just improve your market share.

Promoting yourself online

You need a web presence for your app if you want to provide adequate customer service (more on this in Chapter 21). You should use your web presence to draw customers to your app on the Marketplace.

When you have a web presence, you also can leverage ads on the web. The first rule is to include simple metadata on your pages to attract the search engines — this is search engine optimization (SEO) at its most basic. (For much more information on this subject, turn to *Search Engine Optimization For Dummies,* by Peter Kent [Wiley].)

On a website, you have more real estate than you do within the app description on the Marketplace. Use this space wisely, but don't go into too much detail. You're proud of your work, but you want to leave some mystery for the customers to uncover as they get to know your app.

Don't forget to use social websites: Tweet or post on your Facebook wall. Get your friends to do the same. Consider creating a Wikipedia entry about your app. Comment on blogs and online forums that appeal to your target niche.

Seeking coverage in the press

Get someone else to do your advertising for you. There are bound to be websites, newsletters, and magazines that serve the niche you're serving. Every group of enthusiasts has some means of communicating with other like-minded enthusiasts. Find it, and let the publisher know.

Reporters are always looking for news that is relevant to their audience. They may act aloof, but a story about a smartphone app is exciting news for all but the most jaded users. If you can catch someone's attention, it may pay off. Again, the Internet can provide publicity faster than any other medium.

Also, use press releases when you have news. The focus of the release needs to be on what's new, unique, or otherwise a first. Many readers won't be aware of your app, so you need to talk about what's new rather than what was already available. For more on how to write an effective press release, turn to *Public Relations For Dummies,* 2nd Edition, by Eric Yaverbaum with Bob Bly and Ilise Benun (Wiley).

Pricing your app effectively

The most downloaded apps are free. Giving away your app may be fine if you're feeling altruistic or just starting out. It's also a good way to introduce prospective customers to your approach by offering a trial version, as described earlier in this chapter.

However, if you want a sustainable business model, there needs to be revenue. This means pricing. Pricing your app too high will drive downloads away. Even if your app will make the user $100, charging $20 for it won't likely work.

Most apps are less than $2. The range of $2 to $5 is appropriate for some special apps, mostly established games or products. Anything more than $5 will most likely price you out of the market.

18

Going Global with Your App

In This Chapter

▶ Translating your app for an international audience

▶ Making the right selections in the Marketplace

*W*hen you're ready to take your app outside the United States, you need to consider a number of factors, including language, local laws, cultural norms, and local currency.

Even if your app is a simple widget, it's important to consider how your app will be interpreted in other countries. Neglecting this step could set your app up for failure because the ratings you receive are from all users, both domestic and international. If your app is well received in the United States but offends, say, Canadian sensibilities, your overall ratings will suffer.

Angry users are more likely to leave feedback than satisfied users are.

We start this chapter by looking at the issues you need to consider before taking your app into international markets. Then we cover the mechanics of distributing your app to those markets.

PhotoDisc/Getty Images

Gearing Your App toward an International Audience

Unless you've been involved in product development for a global corporation, you may never have had the challenge of localization. You may, however, have heard any number of amusing stories that have come from earnest but unsuccessful efforts to sell products in other countries. We share some of them here, in the hope that you won't become one of these stories. Following the steps in this chapter will significantly reduce that chance.

Not getting lost in translation

A competitive drinking game on some college campuses involves using a free translation application to convert a sentence to a foreign language and then back to English. If the other person can guess the essence of the unseen original sentence, the person who ran the translations back and forth to English must take a drink.

Here's an example using the automatic translation tools in Microsoft Word to translate a sentence of jargon and then Google Translate to bring it back to English:

> **Before:** Management has partnered to put together a vision post acquisition, which celebrates diversity and incentivizes proactive action items. We will put together to-do lists to get deliverables on the fast lane so we can push the envelope and return to our position as leader in our growth industry.

> **After:** Management has worked to put together a takeover post of vision that celebrates the diversity and incentivizes proactive action items. We will put together to make lists to get final results on the fast lane, so we can push the envelope and return to our position as a leader in our industry on the rise.

Here is what happens when you translate and then retranslate a series of euphemisms:

> **Before:** He was a lousy doctor and many of his patients are pushing up daisies. He was shown the door and now he is in reduced circumstances.

> **After:** He cannot afford a doctor and his patient to push many of the daisy. He made contact and now he is displayed in a simple situation.

The point is that freeware translations are risky and unreliable. Don't rely on such services for your app. At best, the mistranslation will be indecipherable; at worst, it might be unintentionally vulgar or offensive to your audience.

A poor translation shows a lack of diligence. Such mistakes can happen with any translation, but they tend to occur more frequently with non-European languages primarily because of fundamental differences in sentence structure. Perhaps the best-known poor translation in an app was from a war game simulation called Zero Wing that included the following threat from the enemy: "All your base are belong to us." This grammatically tortured sentence turned a challenge into a joke.

You want your app to become famous because it's valuable, not because of a translation mistake. A partial solution to the problem is to review your translation with a native speaker before you publish. However, just working with a native speaker doesn't guarantee that you'll have smooth sailing. There are local dialects that may use different idioms or slang. For example, American English uses idioms completely different from those used in Britain, and vice versa.

Some people recommend using so-called "International English." The idea of International English is that you can write strictly using English words that are universal. The downside of International English is that it tends to strip your writing of colloquialisms and make it seem stilted and formal. Besides, even if you manage to strip out all the idioms, you'll be left with spelling differences. In fact, Windows 2007 accommodates 18 variations of English. Microsoft hires teams of contractors to support the subtle variations of all the different versions of written languages. Windows Phone 7 isn't that sophisticated yet — addressing the variations is up to you.

Do your best to avoid jargon, but keep in mind that you may not be aware of when you're using jargon. (It easily becomes a part of your daily speech.) No translator, free or otherwise, can translate jargon. Your best protection is to have someone from your target audience review your app.

Recognizing local laws

John Perry Barlow, lyricist for the Grateful Dead and founding member of the Electronic Frontier Foundation, has been quoted as saying, "In Cyberspace, the First Amendment is a local ordinance." He recognizes that some U.S. citizens have a difficult time appreciating that the interpretations of the U.S. Constitution — in particular, the Bill of Rights — are not universal rights.

The Microsoft policies that prohibit ridiculing of people or classes of people (see Chapter 16) also have the effect of avoiding the much stricter laws against slander and discrimination.

The kinds of laws that apps sold in international markets are most likely to have issues with are intellectual property laws. When you're developing your app and planning to use licensed code or images, be sure that the license applies in that country. If the license for the image or the code doesn't explicitly apply internationally, it's fair to assume that you don't have permission to use it.

In all likelihood, if you are, indeed, violating your license and you're caught, you'll receive a stern letter from a lawyer requesting that you stop marketing in that or other countries. Unless you're certain that your agreement is valid and you have the advice of an attorney, pull back your app.

Better advice is to plan ahead and get licensing and permissions ahead of time. Don't wait until you're uploading your app to the Marketplace for legal review.

Microsoft application submission rules may help you avoid problems with slander and discrimination, but Microsoft is very careful to leave any licensing issues entirely with you. Along these lines, Microsoft doesn't want to engage in any controversy on the Marketplace, so it'll pull your app quickly if there is a credible accusation that you've cut some corners on obtaining permission. Don't let that happen. Be scrupulous in getting permissions and reading licensing agreements.

Heeding cultural norms

Application logic or images that resonate with you and your friends may generate unexpected reactions in other parts of the world that affect your ratings. Here are some examples of cultural norms within the United States that are not universal and would be a problem in some other countries:

- ✔ **The thumbs-up sign:** You may think of the thumbs-up sign as having positive connotations. Whether it was the Fonz using it in *Happy Days* or the title character using it in *Borat: Cultural Learnings of America for Make Benefit Glorious Nation of Kazakhstan,* the audience knew it was a positive indication. However, the same gesture is the equivalent of giving someone the middle finger in other cultures, including some Spanish-speaking countries.

- ✔ **Skulls:** The presence of skulls in diagrams has lost its meaning within the United States, but some other cultures see it as a powerful symbol of Satanism. You may use a skull and crossbones to gently dissuade people from an area or show what is meant to be a slightly scary pirate or outlaw biker; in other cultures, that symbol would be perceived as much more threatening.

- ✔ **Kicking up your feet:** In the United States, the act of putting one's feet up on a desk shows that the executive is either in control of the situation or that he's relaxing on the job, depending upon the context. This position, which shows other people the soles of your feet, is a grave insult in some cultures and communicates to other in the room that they're beneath contempt.

You can't anticipate every possible reaction in every culture, but awareness of the larger norms is important when planning icons or pictures.

Considering the layout of your app after translation

After you resolve all the cultural and language issues, one technical consideration remains: You carefully prepared the layout to present your words on the Windows Phone screen in your native language, but when you translated the words into another language, the phrases no longer fit in the text boxes you created. This situation is less of a problem if the translation uses less space, but translations often take up more space than the original wording, so you may see words chopped off or hidden.

Be sure to examine each translation's impact on your design, and customize the layout of the app for each language.

Reviewing the International App Submission Process

When you're submitting your app, you need to make a series of selections to properly categorize the app for the international market.

The first submission page is shown in Figure 18-1. Windows Phone supports five languages (six if you count International English):

- ✔ English
- ✔ English (International)
- ✔ French
- ✔ Italian
- ✔ German
- ✔ Spanish

You can offer the option to select dialects within your app, if it helps.

The next place that is relevant for international submission is the pricing page (shown in Figure 18-2). Here, you can select the countries in which you want to market your app. If you want to narrow the options, uncheck the Worldwide Distribution check box and pick which countries you want your app to be available in.

As long as your app isn't free, you can individually select the pricing for each country in that country's local currency.

TIP

Before you submit your app, there are two approaches you can take:

✔ Submit one app that incorporates multiple languages.

✔ Submit a separate app for each language or regional dialect you want to support.

The advantage of submitting one app with multiple languages embedded in it is that you get a much larger download count. The downside is that your app may not translate well, which could result in negative ratings.

Figure 18-1: The first page for submission of your app lets you select the language.

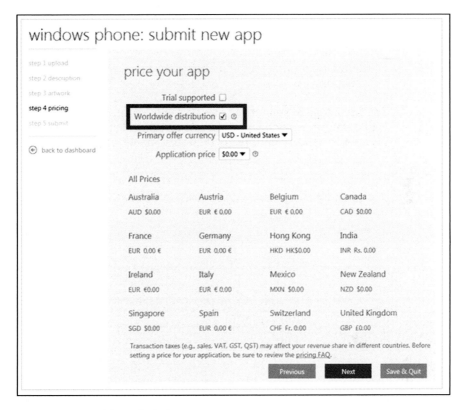

Figure 18-2: The pricing submission page.

19

All This Fun and Getting Paid, Too!

In This Chapter

▶ Tracking your app's sales on the Developer Dashboard

▶ Setting expectations on when you'll get paid

▶ Understanding the Windows Phone Marketplace return policy

*I*f your app is available on the Marketplace for a price, this chapter tells you everything you need to know about getting paid, from tracking your app's sales to knowing when to expect a payment to dealing with returns. We also fill you in on international payments and what those mean for you.

If you've developed your app for the benefit of mankind, and you're not looking to get paid, you can skip this chapter. There is no money in this for you.

Reading the Developer Dashboard

The Developer Dashboard allows you to track how your app is selling on the Marketplace. It provides information such as the number of downloads and, if you're charging for your app, the number you've sold. Also listed is the number of apps that remained sold for more than seven days. The information on the Dashboard is used to calculate the amount of money you've earned.

The Dashboard is broken down into several sections. We walk you through them here.

PhotoDisc, Inc.

Note: Microsoft sometimes updates the layout and sections in the Developer Dashboard, so you may not see the same layout when you log in to App Hub. Whenever there is an update to the Dashboard in the App Hub, you'll receive an e-mail notifying you of the update.

My Apps

The My Apps section of the dashboard is where you can

- ✔ **View all your apps.**

- ✔ **Check the details of each app.** You can see the app's icons, screenshots, and certification status.

- ✔ **Submit new apps.**

- ✔ **Submit updates for your apps when you add new features or fix bugs.**

- ✔ **See whether your e-mail address and publisher identity are verified and confirmed.**

- ✔ **Unlock phones for development, and use them to deploy and test your apps.**

- ✔ **Find out if you're eligible for payout by Microsoft from the sales of your apps.** You'll see one of the following listed for your payout status:

    - **Eligible for Revenue Payout:** This is what you want to see. It means you're all set to receive money.

    - **Pending Eligibility for Revenue Payout:** This message could mean that you haven't made it to the $200 minimum payout or that the payment is still in process.

    - **Not Eligible for Revenue Payout:** This means that something isn't right. For example, it could mean that you closed the bank account you used at registration or some key tax information is missing. The tax information you need to provide if you're in the United States is your Social Security number. If you don't have a Social Security number, you need your Individual Taxpayer Identification Number (ITIN).

        If you aren't based in the United States and have nothing to do with the United States, you're on your own for local taxes. Be aware that the United States has treaties with other countries and shares information on payouts. Talk to a tax specialist in your country to make sure you're paying all appropriate taxes.

My Account

The My Account section displays where you are in terms of personal verification and revenue. This is the part of the process where Microsoft verifies that you are who you say you are.

The My Account section shows the following:

- ✔ **Account Details:** This is where your publisher name, website, e-mail address, postal address, and contact phone number are listed (basically, all the information required of you as a publisher of apps in the Marketplace).

- ✔ **My Profile:** This is the information displayed in your public profile. You can include your website or your company's website, your location, your blog, and forum options (such as content editor and signature).

- ✔ **Payee details:** Here's where you enter your bank details and tax entity type for taxation purposes. Note that you aren't required to add your bank and tax details when you sign up; you can add the details after registration is complete.

- ✔ **Devices:** Here, you see the hardware devices you've registered for testing Windows Phone 7 applications.

- ✔ **Certificates:** Here, you can optionally upload certificates to authenticate requests to the Microsoft Push Notification Service.

In addition, the My Account section displays notifications of any actions concerning your current app submissions. Whenever an app is submitted, these notifications let you know where you are in the submission process. (An e-mail on the status is also sent to your registered e-mail address.)

Reports

The Reports section of the Dashboard is where you can generate reports. For example, you may want to know total downloads in all markets or just the downloads in Norway.

The number of downloads is the total number of people who initially downloaded and/or purchased your app. The important number is the number of people who kept your app for more than seven days. If there is a large difference between the number of downloads and the number of people who kept your app, you need to figure out why.

Your cash balance is the number of purchases minus the returns.

Support

The Support section of the Dashboard allows you to submit a support request to Microsoft regarding your app. When you create a new support request, you'll receive e-mails with regular updates until the issue is resolved.

Knowing When You'll Get Paid

The payout time varies depending on the payment method used by your customers. In general, the collection time is as follows:

- ✔ 15 to 30 days for credit card billing
- ✔ 90 to 120 days for mobile operator billing

You get credit on your Developer Dashboard only when Microsoft has collected money. Microsoft will convert the payments from whatever currency the customer was using to your home currency using a standard foreign exchange rate. (Don't get bogged down in the precise amount of the exchange rate and its fluctuations. Microsoft is fair about this.)

Microsoft pays developers when they are owed more than $200. The payment frequency may vary depending on the earnings of the developer. You get 70 percent of the sale price of your app, and Microsoft gets the other 30 percent.

When you registered for a Windows Live ID and registered as a developer, you provided your bank account information. If Microsoft tries to pay you, and your account is closed, Microsoft won't keep the cash from you, but you may need to provide extra verification that the new account is valid. Microsoft doesn't want to get into any controversy in which Partner A of the publisher gets in a dispute with Partner B and changes the payments from the partnership's account to his personal account. Do yourself and Microsoft a favor, and be prepared to show justification that your bank account is changing. Microsoft will just let the money pile up rather than get into a lawsuit.

Accepting the Liberal Return Policies of the Marketplace

Microsoft's return policies for apps is very liberal — anyone who buys an app can return it (actually, surrender his license to it) within seven days, no questions asked. The good news about this is that more people will download your app — they're more willing to download an app when they know they can return it if it doesn't live up to their expectations.

It pays to have a website associated with your app to answer frequently asked questions (see Chapter 21). This way, people can read up on your app before they buy, so they know exactly what you provide.

The better your app, the lower your return rate. One way to avoid returns is to offer two versions of your app: a free version with limited functions or a limited number of uses and a full-featured pay version. People will be more likely to download the free version first and download the fee-based version only if they really want it.

Although you can give away your app for free, the least you can charge for your app is 99¢. The most you can charge is $499. And, in the current version of the Marketplace, you can charge only a one-time fee. There is no option for a recurring subscription fee. A subscription model may be available at some point — and that'll be good news for some apps and bad for others. Many customers hesitate to pay a large upfront fee. Paying more on a monthly basis for an app that they use routinely can be a good solution for users (and developers benefit from that setup, too).

Part VI

A Designer's Work Is Never Done: Updates and Customer Service

In this part . . .

Writing and then launching your first app is a big deal, but it's only the beginning. You need to offer ongoing updates of bug fixes and new features just to keep up with your competition.

In addition, you need to support your customers — answering their questions about your app and helping them troubleshoot when things don't go as planned. Sure, Microsoft requires you to offer customer support, but it's in your best interest to do so — if you don't provide good customer support, your reputation will be shot.

Photo credits: PhotoDisc/Getty Images (top, bottom); PhotoDisc, Inc. (middle)

20

Updating Your App

Many novice programmers learn the hard way that their first submission is not their last. It's very satisfying to get to the point where you submit your work, but that's only the beginning of an extended process of bug fixes, revisions, and enhancements.

There are many reasons to update your app:

- ✔ To fix bugs
- ✔ To refresh the user interface
- ✔ To add features to outpace the competition or to stay competitive
- ✔ To add languages or dialects
- ✔ To respond to changes Microsoft made to the APIs
- ✔ To respond to customer feedback
- ✔ To enhance performance

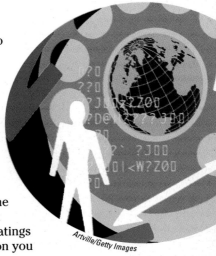

Artville/Getty Images

In this chapter, we fill you in on how often to update your app and the mechanics of actually submitting the update. No matter how great your app is, if you don't update it regularly, you'll lose customers, and your ratings will suffer. In this chapter, we give you the information you need to keep your app on top for years to come.

Setting the Timing of Updates

How often you should update your app is dependent on a variety of other factors, including the need to be available at key release dates like conventions or sporting events, competitive releases, and the demands or expectations of your sources of funding.

Among professional developers, there are two strategies to managing the timing of new releases: the waterfall method and the agile software method. Either of these approaches could justify its own book, but here's a brief description:

- ✔ **The waterfall method:** In the waterfall method, you create a well-defined road map of new features, capabilities, and bug fixes. You carefully define the new feature set and set a schedule based upon your best estimate of how fast you can develop, test, and document the release. If you're part of a large organization, your sales and marketing teams can develop plans based upon the release of new features.

  Under the waterfall approach, the feature set of the new release is what matters most. The delivery schedule can slip (within reason).

- ✔ **The agile software method:** This approach, also called the scrum method, switches the primary focus from the feature delivery and bug fixes to the delivery schedule. Here, you have a prioritized list of items to address, but the schedule is sacrosanct and doesn't move (again, within reason). If a release does not address a prioritized feature or bug in the upcoming release, it's moved to the next release.

The approach that's best for you depends upon your style, the competitive situation, and customer preferences:

- ✔ **Your style:** If you're the kind of person who operates well on a fixed schedule, and you like the idea of being able to plan for releases every month or every three months or however often is necessary, the agile software method is the one for you. On the other hand, if you don't live and die by a calendar, and features are where your focus is, the waterfall method will meet your needs.

- ✔ **The competitive situation:** If your competition updates its apps on a regular schedule, you may find that you need to follow suit and use the waterfall method. On the other hand, if you use the agile software method, you can shake things up within the industry by announcing your feature releases just before or just after your competition.

✔ **Customer preferences:** If your target customers want it all and want it now, like many consumers, the faster you can get attractive features to market, the more competitive you are; this model is suitable for the agile software method of development. On the other hand, if your customers are hierarchical organizations that will be integrating your app into a complex system in an orderly fashion, they'll prefer to work with the waterfall method because it's more predictable and integrates more easily into a schedule. Such organizations dislike schedule slips, but they *despise* not knowing which features they can have in an upcoming release. If a release is de-featured, who really knows when the feature they're seeking will really be available?

What you don't want to do is a hybrid of the two strategies — instead of getting the best of both worlds, you end up with the worst: The feature set is reduced, and the dates slip.

Reviewing the Resubmission Process

Microsoft expects you to update your app, and the Dashboard allows you to update your app with minimal fuss. The good news: You can submit updates to your apps at no cost to you. The not-so-good news: You can't charge users for an application update.

Submitting an update to Microsoft

We cover the process for submitting version 1.0 of your app in Chapter 16. The process for submitting a new revision or version is similar.

Figure 20-1 shows the first page of the application submission. Here, you can see the version number; the default setting is 1.0. To increment the next release, you set the Version to 1.1 if you're just uploading a revision or 2.0 if you've created a whole new version of your app (see the "Talking the revision control talk" sidebar for more on the difference).

This page is where you upload the new XAP package. It goes through the same approval process that your original app went through. You'll need to include icons, a description, and all the other elements (see Chapter 16).

Make sure that your description clearly outlines what the new revision or version includes so that your customers know what they're getting. Talk about how much better this revision or version is. ***Remember:*** You're still looking for new users. Look at your original description, and make sure you include those same selling points in your new description.

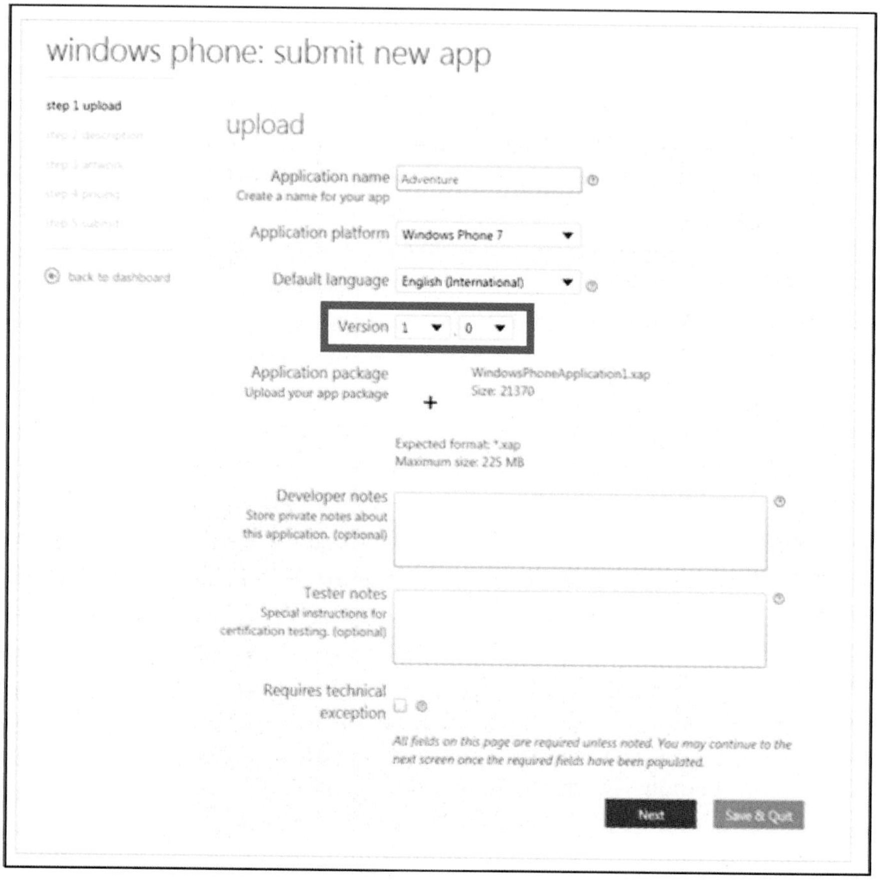

Figure 20-1: The first step for application submission.

Getting your update to your customers

Simply resubmitting your app is enough to offer your users the update. Each time a user launches your app, the Windows Phone checks with the Marketplace to verify that the license is valid and that the user has the most recent revision. If not, the user receives a notification of an update.

You can let this process just happen. But your new release is an opportunity to communicate with your customers and tell them how good you are. You have a captive audience, and because they like your app enough to launch it, it's fair to assume that they have a favorable impression of your work. Even if they have little choice, you can take this opportunity to convince them that they can't live without your updated app.

Talking the revision control talk

Some people have spent their careers defining the lexicon used to describe different software releases. Here are the terms you need to know:

- **Release:** A *release* is any update of software, large or small. As long as it's different from an earlier release, it's considered a new release.

- **Revision:** A *revision* is an enhancement to an earlier version. In general, the first release of an app is called 1.0. The next enhancement is revision 1.1, the one after that is 1.2, and so on.

Most users will expect that they can use files created with earlier revisions with a new revision (known as *backward compatibility*). The old files may not be able to take advantage of all the new capabilities of the new revision; for example, if the application is a game, the user can expect that the new revision will keep track of his previous scores.

- **Version:** A new *version* of a software package offers users a significant enhancement. Typically, new iconography and a new user interface are created to go along with a new version. In addition to the superficial aspects, there should be significant new functionality that adds value for users in order for it to be considered a new version.

You don't have to rely on the Marketplace to tell your customers about your update. Send e-mails to all your users. Put a notification on your website. Send out a press release. Share the news with blogs that might be interested in posting about your update. If the update is a big improvement, you may get some new users from word of mouth.

21

Supporting Your End-Users

You can put an app on the Marketplace and do nothing more . . . almost. During the submission process, you're asked to provide an e-mail address for technical support (see Figure 21-1).

Technically, you don't *have* to provide an e-mail address at this point in the submission process, but Microsoft requires that application developers provide technical support to users. They leave it up to you precisely how you want to provide that service — the only requirement is that it be "easily discoverable."

Users will have questions, even with the simplest app. Providing support will improve the likelihood that customers will keep your app, rate it highly, and recommend it to their friends. Plus, providing good support will improve your reputation and make it more likely that users will buy other apps you develop down the road.

There are three levels of customer support:

© IT Stock

✔ Minimalist support, which complies with Microsoft's requirements but doesn't do anything else

✔ Standard support, which seeks to address any concerns at a manageable cost

✔ Concierge-level support, which seeks to make service a point of competitive differentiation

We cover all three levels of support in this chapter.

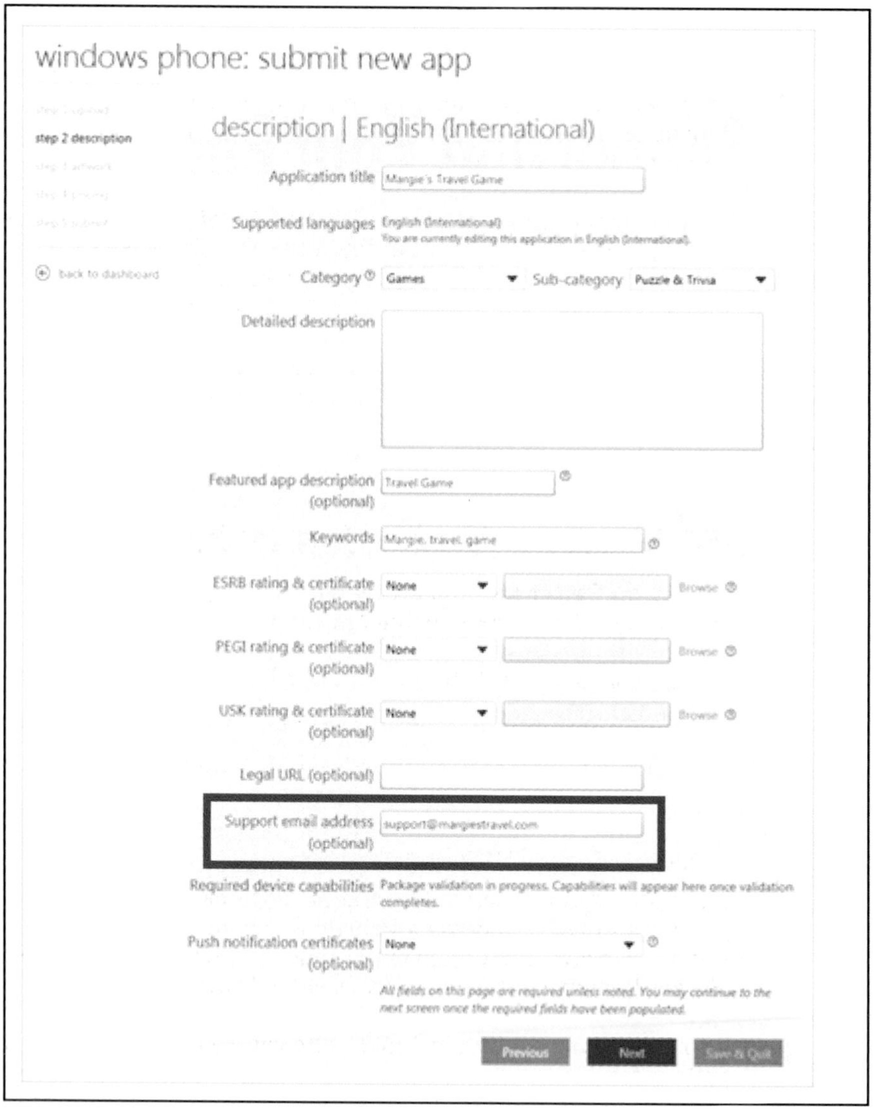

Figure 21-1: This is where you specify your support e-mail address.

Meeting Your Obligations to Provide Customer Support

You *could* list your personal e-mail address or phone number for customer support. These are good options if you never sleep and are eager to answer questions at all hours of the day and night.

A better option is to create a new e-mail address for customer support. You don't have to spend any money on this — you can use a free web-based e-mail service like Hotmail, Gmail, or Yahoo! Mail. If you don't want to use your own name in the e-mail address, try choosing an address that corresponds to the name of your app (for example, `sampleappcustomer service@hotmail.com`).

Try to respond within 24 hours of the receipt of an e-mail. If you're the one providing all customer service, check the account regularly, maybe several times a day (including weekends and holidays). Customer service never sleeps. The cost of letting an inquiry fester too long? Negative ratings.

You may feel like you're getting back to people quickly, but when someone is having a problem with your app, half a day may feel like an eternity. The sooner you can reply, the better.

Standard Options for Customer Service

Beyond the basics (see the preceding section), there are three mainstream options for offering your customers support:

- ✓ Establishing a website
- ✓ Creating videos to show how to use your app on sites like YouTube
- ✓ Creating a presence on an existing social-networking site like Facebook

Creating a website for your app

For anything more than the most basic app, the current standard of care is to provide a website. Building a website is beyond the scope of this book, but if you want to create one from the ground up, we recommend, *Building a Web Site For Dummies,* 4th Edition, by David A. Crowder (Wiley).

If you don't want to have to build a site yourself, look into some affordable options for designing websites using templates. For example, Virb (`www. virb.com`) offers websites for $10 per month, and you can customize existing templates to make the site fit your needs.

The domain name for your site should include the name of the app (for example, `sampleapp.com`). Another possibility, if you think you might create multiple apps sooner rather than later, is to name your app design business, register that domain name (for example, `yourappdesignbusiness.com`), and create separate pages on your site for each of your apps (for example, `www.yourappdesignbusiness.com/sampleapp1`, `www.yourappdesign business.com/sampleapp2`, and so on).

Regardless of how you set up your site, it should include the following:

✔ **A detailed description of the application:** You have 50 words and eight bullet points to describe your app within the Marketplace. Compare this to a website, where there is no practical limit to the amount of detail you can provide.

Providing more detailed information on your app has many benefits, including setting realistic expectations about what your app can and can't do. This, in turn, reduces the number of inquiries you'll receive from customers. Plus, it will help your ratings because prospective customers will have a better appreciation of the capabilities of your app and won't buy it if it doesn't do what they want.

✔ **An FAQ section:** You can save yourself a lot of time answering e-mails if you prepare responses in anticipation of questions you can expect. Add to this list as you start seeing the same questions from numerous customers. Not sure which questions your customers will have? Look around at other apps' FAQs, and see if any of those might apply to your app. Here's an example of the FAQs for the app Shazam: www.shazam. com/music/web/faqs.html?platform=wp7.

✔ **A basic user's guide:** Your website can offer a user's guide and a quick start guide. The user's guide is a complete set of instructions for the app; the quick start guide is an abbreviated version, telling the users just what they need to know to get started.

Preparing user documentation has two primary benefits to you:

• Some users are comfortable reading user documentation. This will eliminate your need to provide them any technical support — they'll find the answers they need in the documentation.

• The documentation gives you a place to refer the users who do contact you for technical support.

You may consider the app simple to use, but chances are, you've been spending your nights and weekends putting this together, so you know it inside and out. Your users will be coming to it fresh, and they may have questions.

✔ **Customer support contact information:** E-mail is the easiest way for customers to contact you. Provide a link to your e-mail address from your website and/or from within your app.

As you start getting questions from customers, prepare stock answers to send out. That way, whenever someone e-mails you to ask a particular question, you can copy and paste your stock response, saving yourself

> some time. Occasionally, someone will ask a question you've never
> heard before, or they'll need help that a stock response won't cover; in
> those cases, you'll want to spend more time customizing a response.

✔ **Advertising:** You can offer a valuable service to your customers if you
provide them information from highly targeted advertisers. As long as
you're careful and truly serve your audience, they won't consider the
ads intrusive.

Putting together video demonstrations

Some people are comfortable reading a manual, but others do better if they
can see what they're supposed to do. If you prefer, you can post your videos
on your website, but a better option may be to upload them to YouTube.
That way, you can still embed them in your website, but your audience might
be a bit bigger.

You don't need expensive technology to create a serviceable YouTube video.
You should, however, write a script for your presentation so that you come
off sounding polished and professional.

If you aren't happy with the quality of the video you come up with, you can
hire a pro to shoot one for you. A professionally developed video can cost
several thousand dollars per minute.

Tapping into social networks

Don't forget to set up a Facebook page and Twitter account for your app —
and be sure to update them regularly. This gives fans of your app a place to
share information and build a community. And it gives you a way to communicate with users and prospective users directly, outside the Marketplace.

Concierge-Level Support

When we say "concierge-level support," we're talking about offering excep-
tional customer care as a way to differentiate your app from your competitors.

You aren't allowed to charge for enhanced service as a subscription through
the Marketplace. As of this writing, it's unclear whether you're prohibited
from enhancing the relationship with your users by charging a subscription
fee through your website. When in doubt, reread the Marketplace Terms of
Service at `http://create.msdn.com`.

Enhancing your website

You can enhance your users' experience by offering the following on your site:

- **Live chat:** When you reach a critical mass, you'll need to hire a full-time customer service rep. (When you're just starting out as a developer, this is only a dream. But this kind of demand can sneak up on you, even with moderate success.) Live chat is a way for your customer service rep(s) to be more efficient: A proficient agent can handle up to six simultaneous conversations on live chat.

- **Registration:** Most of your communication with users is best done though the Marketplace — it's a surefire way to communicate with every active user. However, some users may want to affiliate with your app by registering on your website. If you offer them some enhanced value — such as the opportunity to provide feedback, get product updates, and join a community of like-minded users — you can collect useful information about them.

  If you collect information about users, you have an obligation to protect their privacy, in addition to publishing and maintaining a privacy policy.

- **A web-based version of your app:** Offering a web-based version of your app is mostly a matter of reformatting a Silverlight app for a full PC screen (see Chapter 7). Users get comfortable with a user interface, and if they like your app on their phones, they'll like it on their PCs.

  When you offer a web-based version of your app, users may find you through the Marketplace or through your website. In other words, your web-based app may pull them in to your phone-based app, and your phone-based app may pull them in to your web-based app. Either way, you increase your presence, which is a great way to outpace your competition.

Integrating support within your app

You can build some basic customer support into your app. It's standard practice for PC applications to offer online support and even context-aware help. Such assistance is less common for mobile apps, so it may be what sets your app apart.

Integrated support can come in several forms:

- A basic user's guide that is accessible from within your app
- Links to your website, particularly the FAQ section
- Live chat via texting
- E-mail support linked to the e-mail service on the Windows Phone
- Community support via a social-networking site such as Facebook

Part VII
The Part of Tens

Courtesy of Microsoft Corporation

In this part . . .

When you're short on time, and you still want a lot of bang for your buck, this is the part for you.

Here, we fill you in on ten features that the Windows Phone should and may have in its next release. Just as you'll be regularly enhancing your app, Microsoft plans to make the platform better in the months and years ahead. In this part, we tell you what to anticipate.

We also bring together in one place the ten (or so) steps to make your app as popular as possible.

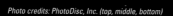

Photo credits: PhotoDisc, Inc. (top, middle, bottom)

Ten Features to Look for Down the Road

*T*he Windows Phone 7 we describe in this book is the first major iteration of the platform. Although there is a long legacy on the Windows CE platform, much of what you see in the initial release is new. In addition, it was pushed into the market before everything could be ready. So, although it's a great platform, we've come up with ten features that you can expect to see down the road.

Getting Oriented with a Compass

The current version of the Windows Phone doesn't support a compass. Although the phone is able to find its location on the map, it can't tell you in which direction you're heading. Ideally, when you turn, the orientation of the map would change, but as of this writing, this doesn't happen. When this capability is properly supported, the Windows Phone will be able to give users better directions.

PhotoDisc, Inc.

Side-Loading Files and Applications

Side-loading an application means connecting the cellphone to a computer with a USB cable and being able to install files and apps from the computer onto the phone. Currently, the only way to download music, Microsoft Office files, and images is wirelessly. Microsoft has made the downloading as convenient as possible, but sometimes users want the control that they can get with side-loading. Downloading via a USB cable is faster than downloading wirelessly, which is especially important if you're moving a lot of data. Plus, we got this capability on Windows Mobile 6.X and had to give it up with Windows Phone 7.

Side-loading presents some risks when it comes to the stability of a phone. Microsoft is concerned that apps could be installed on the phone that haven't gone through the approval process. This could include spyware, malware, or apps that access functions without notifying the user.

However, it's a hassle for programmers like us to have to debug applications only with an emulator. Even if the emulator were perfect (which isn't the case), there would be value from testing on a unit you can carry with you. It'll be nice when Microsoft allows the side-loading capability with all the necessary security it insists upon.

Multitasking

The current Windows Phone 7 operating system allows only one application to function at a time. The user can answer an incoming phone call in the middle of using an app, but having to open and close apps all the time is inconvenient. Windows Phone 7 may allow this kind of flexibility at some point, possibly by the end of 2011.

Accessing Shared Data on the Phone

Currently, any file that you open on the Windows Phone is usable only by a single application. There is no support for shared files outside the sandbox.

This is a big problem for Microsoft Office files. SharePoint begins to address this problem, but it isn't the complete solution. The reason for not allowing an app to work with other files is primarily data security. For example, you wouldn't want to have an app manipulating the contact database on the phone in case the app contains malware.

Microsoft will address this issue sooner or later. We hope sooner.

Supporting Native Applications

Currently, all apps on Windows Phone 7 must work within the sandbox. Again, this is one of the compromises that Microsoft made to speed availability of the new platform.

Frankly, managed code on a fast processor like that present on the Windows Phone is more than adequate for most applications. However, some apps that demand faster response — like VoIP and videoconferencing — do not run well in a managed sandbox.

If carriers don't want that class of application because it uses too many of their resources or cannibalizes the revenue for a service they offer, that's a choice they can make. However, preventing all performance-based applications overreaches. We think that both the Windows Phone Marketplace and the marketplace in general should determine which apps are viable.

Supporting Adobe Flash

The first iteration of Windows Phone 7 doesn't support Adobe Flash. This means that many popular websites won't run properly.

There is no need to build support for Adobe Flash. Microsoft will be enabling this capability in 2011.

Integrating with Office Mobile

One of the drawbacks to Windows Phone is that you have to enter all your data on the phone. Previous systems have allowed the use of Office Mobile, which allows you to use Microsoft Office to access e-mail, schedule appointments, and see the contact list that you've entered on your computer. Syncing your computer with your phone allows the PC and the phone to have the same information. The current setup requires that all information be passed through the cellular carrier.

Outputting to an External Monitor

Some phones currently allow you to connect your phone to an external monitor. The advantage of having a larger screen means less panning with bigger and more detailed graphics.

Being able to connect your Windows Phone to drive an HDTV will be very convenient. It'll expand the value of the phone by supporting a larger screen and allow for apps that can exploit a high-resolution screen with more immersive graphics.

Inputting with an External Keyboard

When you add an external keyboard to the external monitor, you're really opening up new possibilities. Maybe you have tiny fingers and thumbs and can type as fast on the virtual keyboard as you can on an external keyboard. But for the rest of us, the capability of hooking up a real QWERTY keyboard would be a true advantage. This makes the phone a functional portable computer, allowing you to leave your PC at home when you travel.

Creating More Prewritten Code Samples

As of this writing, there are fewer than 100 prewritten code samples. This number will grow over time, but having more code samples would be valuable. Maybe you could offer up some sample code, too. Of course, you only get bragging rights — no cash.

Supporting Mobile Device Management

In rough numbers, about two-thirds of all phones used in the United States are at least occasionally used for business purposes. Some are provided by a company for its mobile employees. Others allow their employees to get their own phones. Of these, some employees get reimbursed, while others make business calls at their own expense.

Regardless of who pays, a large number of smartphone users are accessing corporate information — contacts or e-mails or super-secret files with financial forecasts.

Here's our point: After a company allows corporate information to go onto a phone, it has a responsibility to protect that information, no matter who owns the phone.

This is one of the functions of a class of applications called Mobile Device Management (MDM). Good MDM software knows who has downloaded what information to what device, and what level of security is turned on and set properly for this phone, if any.

The problem is that MDM software can't do this very effectively when the only apps you can add can run only in a sandbox. Without MDM, many companies will opt to use other phones.

Ten (Or So) Ways to Make Your App More Successful

*T*here are two ways to measure the success of an application. If the app is free and does not include ads, success is measured by the number of downloads. If the app is available for a fee or supported by ads, success is measured by its profitability. Either way, this chapter presents a variety of ways you can make your app more successful.

Of course, this assumes that you're interested in measuring your success by one of these traditional standards, and this may not be the case. You may be completely satisfied with the pure joy of writing code or the praise you get from users. If that's the case, this chapter isn't for you. Go forth and write code!

However, if you want to be more successful using the traditional measures, read on.

PhotoDisc, Inc.

Looking at the App from the User's Perspective

When you put an application out in the Windows Phone Marketplace, you're putting the best you have out there. By the time your app is in the Marketplace, you've planned, programmed, troubleshot, set up customer services, and designed.

And then some random customer spends two seconds looking at the results from a search in the Marketplace hub (see Figure 23-1), and chooses your competitor's app because he likes the name better, or because he likes the app icon better, or because the other app has more downloads because it's been on the Marketplace longer.

All these possibilities are the reality of app marketing. You can either give up now (not recommended) or step up and accept the challenge. You do the latter by looking at the buying process of a lightly interested consumer.

Sure, you've been living and breathing this app for weeks or months, but try imagining downloading the app yourself. Does it do what you say it does in your description? Is it easy to use? Are there any features that seem unnecessary? Is the icon as catchy as it could be?

Figure 23-1: The full panorama of the Marketplace hub.

You may want to solicit feedback about your app from potential users. One way to do this is to release an early version without much fanfare and have a few dozen friends and family members take a look. A more sophisticated approach is to contact a random sampling of the target market and solicit their input in a focus group for a small honorarium ($20 or so per person).

Taking Your Silverlight Work to the Web

A web presence will help you market your app and provide customer support. With the tools that are available today, building and maintaining a website can be simple.

This book shows you how to use Silverlight to make your app. But Silverlight was initially designed to make exciting web pages. Building your web page using Silverlight will make your website more attractive to your customers. You have the tools. You have the skills. Use these to build a web page that provides customer service for your mobile app.

Heck, take it a step further: Make a web-based version of your app. That way, your customers can use the web-based version when they're at their desks and the mobile version when they're on the go. Depending upon the app, that just might be the feature you need to achieve success.

Refer to Chapter 7 to find out more about Silverlight.

Taking Your XNA Work to the Xbox

This book focuses on using Silverlight, but you may have been writing your application in XNA. If so, you can adapt it for the Xbox — the same code will work on the game system. And you can increase the screen size and resolution. Expanding your market to include Xbox opens up a whole new market.

You also can do the opposite: If you're already an Xbox developer, use this book to modify your Xbox applications for the smaller but much more mobile Windows Phone 7. You already have a reputation among your existing customers — give them more opportunities to play your stellar game.

Taking Your Storyboards to Other Platforms

The carefully constructed storyboards that you used to construct your app include your screen layouts and logical flow. Guess what? This work is probably adaptable to other cellphone operating systems.

Forget about loyalty. Your loyalty should be focused on your target customers. If they're demonstrably loyal to the Windows Phone 7 platform, all right then — focus your efforts on continuously improving your app on this one platform. Of course, this will be a rare exception (unless you're targeting Microsoft employees, for example). Even then, there are troublemakers and iconoclasts in Redmond who insist on using non-Microsoft products.

The fact of the matter is, unless you become wildly successful, Microsoft won't even notice if you were less than perfectly loyal to its platform. Besides, unless you make some sort of agreement with Microsoft, you're perfectly free to take your intellectual property anywhere you want. Have at it!

When it comes to alternatives, Apple's iPhone and the Android platform are getting the most press. But don't forget BlackBerry — even though it's no longer the dominant smartphone platform, it still has a loyal following.

For more information, check out the following Wiley Publishing titles: *iPhone Application Development For Dummies,* 3rd Edition, by Neal Goldstein; *Android Application Development For Dummies,* by Donn Felker; and *BlackBerry Application Development For Dummies,* by Karl G. Kowalski.

Expanding Your Marketing Budget

Marketing has the potential to increase your bottom line — it just has to be applied the right way.

The first step is to know your target market. If you have nothing more specific than "My target is the people who want my app," your only option is to advertise to the mass market and hope something sticks. But if you know your audience well — for example, you know that your target audience are parents between the ages of 28 and 42, with school-age children — you could find ways to advertise to that group of people.

Marketing is a big topic, beyond the scope of this book. But if you're looking for more information, check out *Guerrilla Marketing For Dummies,* by Jonathan Margolis and Patrick Garrigan (Wiley). It's chock-full of innovative strategies for getting the word out about your product.

Planning for Enhancements and Upgrades

Whatever your app does, and however much effort you put into your app, you'll discover new features to include. The market changes over time. New apps may come in and surpass yours. You need to watch the market and adapt by adding new features.

Pay attention to the comments you get on your app, both on the Windows Phone Marketplace and on your website. Sure, some people are out for blood — and you can ignore them. But most customers are sincere — even if you don't like the message, you should accept the comments as constructive criticism.

Watch the competition. You want to be able to say that you're the best, but you can't make that claim if you don't know your competition.

When you have an enhancement or an upgrade, take the opportunity to market it to your customers — both the installed base and your target market. The tools we cover in Chapter 20 make it as easy as possible to relaunch the new-and-improved version of your app.

Focusing on Customer Service

Good customer service will not only keep your current app users happy, but also improve your reputation. If your users receive good customer service, they're more likely to purchase your other apps and tell their friends. On the flip side, if your users are treated poorly, your reputation will suffer.

You know from your own experience as a customer how you feel when you're treated well by a company. That's the same feeling you want to foster in your customers. When in doubt, treat your customers the way you would want to be treated, and you won't go wrong.

Make sure that your website clearly displays all the apps you offer so that users of one app will know to try another.

Considering "For Free" and "For Fee" Offerings

Even if your major motivation for writing an app is to make money, offering a free version of your app may be a wise move. The free version gives users the option to try a limited version of your app. If you have two versions of your app — one free and one for a fee — you may increase your total sales.

You can pull them in with the free version — tease them with some value, but don't satisfy them with the whole experience. Then, when they get frustrated and want the full-featured version, they'll buy your app, not your competition's.

Some customers actively seek out apps with a free version so they can get more direct experience before buying.

Having Fun

You probably won't get rich writing apps. So, you may as well have fun with it! If developing an app isn't fun, why bother? Plus, if you have fun with your app, your attitude will shine through. And having fun really is the true measure of success.

Index

Apple & Macs

iPad For Dummies
978-0-470-58027-1

iPhone For Dummies,
4th Edition
978-0-470-87870-5

MacBook For Dummies, 3rd
Edition
978-0-470-76918-8

Mac OS X Snow Leopard For
Dummies
978-0-470-43543-4

Business

Bookkeeping For Dummies
978-0-7645-9848-7

Job Interviews
For Dummies,
3rd Edition
978-0-470-17748-8

Resumes For Dummies,
5th Edition
978-0-470-08037-5

Starting an
Online Business
For Dummies,
6th Edition
978-0-470-60210-2

Stock Investing
For Dummies,
3rd Edition
978-0-470-40114-9

Successful
Time Management
For Dummies
978-0-470-29034-7

Computer Hardware

BlackBerry
For Dummies,
4th Edition
978-0-470-60700-8

Computers For Seniors
For Dummies,
2nd Edition
978-0-470-53483-0

PCs For Dummies, Windows
7 Edition
978-0-470-46542-4

Laptops For Dummies,
4th Edition
978-0-470-57829-2

Cooking & Entertaining

Cooking Basics
For Dummies,
3rd Edition
978-0-7645-7206-7

Wine For Dummies,
4th Edition
978-0-470-04579-4

Diet & Nutrition

Dieting For Dummies,
2nd Edition
978-0-7645-4149-0

Nutrition For Dummies,
4th Edition
978-0-471-79868-2

Weight Training
For Dummies,
3rd Edition
978-0-471-76845-6

Digital Photography

Digital SLR Cameras &
Photography For Dummies,
3rd Edition
978-0-470-46606-3

Photoshop Elements 8
For Dummies
978-0-470-52967-6

Gardening

Gardening Basics
For Dummies
978-0-470-03749-2

Organic Gardening
For Dummies,
2nd Edition
978-0-470-43067-5

Green/Sustainable

Raising Chickens
For Dummies
978-0-470-46544-8

Green Cleaning
For Dummies
978-0-470-39106-8

Health

Diabetes For Dummies,
3rd Edition
978-0-470-27086-8

Food Allergies
For Dummies
978-0-470-09584-3

Living Gluten-Free
For Dummies,
2nd Edition
978-0-470-58589-4

Hobbies/General

Chess For Dummies,
2nd Edition
978-0-7645-8404-6

Drawing
Cartoons & Comics
For Dummies
978-0-470-42683-8

Knitting For Dummies,
2nd Edition
978-0-470-28747-7

Organizing
For Dummies
978-0-7645-5300-4

Su Doku For Dummies
978-0-470-01892-7

Home Improvement

Home Maintenance
For Dummies,
2nd Edition
978-0-470-43063-7

Home Theater
For Dummies,
3rd Edition
978-0-470-41189-6

Living the
Country Lifestyle
All-in-One
For Dummies
978-0-470-43061-3

Solar Power Your Home
For Dummies,
2nd Edition
978-0-470-59678-4

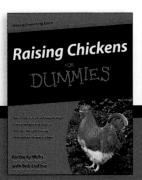

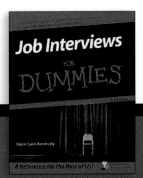

Internet

Blogging For Dummies,
3rd Edition
978-0-470-61996-4

eBay For Dummies,
6th Edition
978-0-470-49741-8

Facebook For Dummies, 3rd
Edition
978-0-470-87804-0

Web Marketing
For Dummies,
2nd Edition
978-0-470-37181-7

WordPress
For Dummies,
3rd Edition
978-0-470-59274-8

Language & Foreign Language

French For Dummies
978-0-7645-5193-2

Italian Phrases
For Dummies
978-0-7645-7203-6

Spanish For Dummies,
2nd Edition
978-0-470-87855-2

Spanish For Dummies,
Audio Set
978-0-470-09585-0

Math & Science

Algebra I For Dummies,
2nd Edition
978-0-470-55964-2

Biology For Dummies,
2nd Edition
978-0-470-59875-7

Calculus For Dummies
978-0-7645-2498-1

Chemistry For Dummies
978-0-7645-5430-8

Microsoft Office

Excel 2010 For Dummies
978-0-470-48953-6

Office 2010 All-in-One
For Dummies
978-0-470-49748-7

Office 2010 For Dummies,
Book + DVD Bundle
978-0-470-62698-6

Word 2010 For Dummies
978-0-470-48772-3

Music

Guitar For Dummies,
2nd Edition
978-0-7645-9904-0

iPod & iTunes
For Dummies,
8th Edition
978-0-470-87871-2

Piano Exercises
For Dummies
978-0-470-38765-8

Parenting & Education

Parenting For Dummies,
2nd Edition
978-0-7645-5418-6

Type 1 Diabetes
For Dummies
978-0-470-17811-9

Pets

Cats For Dummies,
2nd Edition
978-0-7645-5275-5

Dog Training For Dummies,
3rd Edition
978-0-470-60029-0

Puppies For Dummies,
2nd Edition
978-0-470-03717-1

Religion & Inspiration

The Bible For Dummies
978-0-7645-5296-0

Catholicism For Dummies
978-0-7645-5391-2

Women in the Bible
For Dummies
978-0-7645-8475-6

Self-Help & Relationship

Anger Management
For Dummies
978-0-470-03715-7

Overcoming Anxiety
For Dummies,
2nd Edition
978-0-470-57441-6

Sports

Baseball
For Dummies,
3rd Edition
978-0-7645-7537-2

Basketball
For Dummies,
2nd Edition
978-0-7645-5248-9

Golf For Dummies,
3rd Edition
978-0-471-76871-5

Web Development

Web Design
All-in-One
For Dummies
978-0-470-41796-6

Web Sites
Do-It-Yourself
For Dummies,
2nd Edition
978-0-470-56520-9

Windows 7

Windows 7
For Dummies
978-0-470-49743-2

Windows 7
For Dummies,
Book + DVD Bundle
978-0-470-52398-8

Windows 7 All-in-One
For Dummies
978-0-470-48763-1

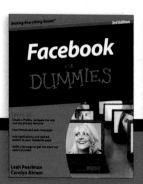
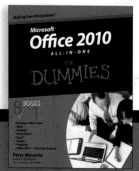

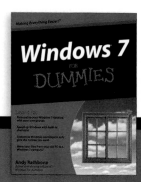

Available wherever books are sold. For more information or to order direct: U.S. customers visit www.dummies.com or call 1-877-762-297
U.K. customers visit www.wileyeurope.com or call (0) 1243 843291. Canadian customers visit www.wiley.ca or call 1-800-567-4797.

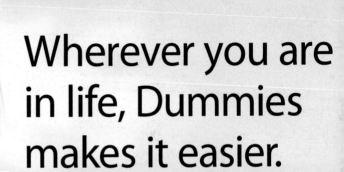